Hacking AI: Adversarial Attacks, Security Risks, and Defense Strategies

OrangeBooks Publication

1st Floor, Rajhans Arcade, Mall Road, Kohka, Bhilai, Chhattisgarh 490020

Website: **www.orangebooks.in**

First Edition, 2025

ISBN: 978-93-6554-009-3

Price: Rs. 399.00

Printed in India

HACKING AI

ADVERSARIAL ATTACKS SECURITY RISKS AND DEFENSE STRATEGIES

DINESH BESIAHGARI | KRISHNA KANDI

OrangeBooks Publication
www.orangebooks.in

About the Author

Dinesh Besiahgari

Dinesh Besiahgari is a globally recognized technologist, author, and innovation leader at Amazon Web Services. With multiple patents and 15+ research papers, his work spans AI, cloud security, and large-scale system design. He's the author of Hacking AI: Adversarial Attacks, Security Risks, and Defense Strategies and co-founder of Ticketsque. Featured in Forbes and Business Insider, Dinesh mentors young engineers, judges global tech competitions, and champions ethical innovation. His leadership combines technical depth with purpose-driven impact. Through every role, he stays focused on building technology that uplifts people and solves real-world problems.

Krishna Kandi

Krishna Kandi is a senior software engineer with 20+ years of experience in FinTech, VoIP software development, Data Engineering, and Cybersecurity. Specializing in AI security, he has worked on securing financial systems, fortifying VoIP applications, and leveraging data-driven security strategies. As a co-author of Hacking AI: Adversarial Attacks, Security Risks, and Defense Strategies, he explores adversarial AI, cybersecurity threats, and defense mechanisms. He is also a member of IEEE.

Dedicated Reviewer Credits

Dr. Manjunath Kounte is currently working as Professor and Head of Electronics and Computer Engineering at REVA University, Bengaluru, India. With over 17 years of experience in teaching, research, and administration, he holds a Bachelor's in Electronics and Communication Engineering, a Master's in Computer Network Engineering from VTU Belagavi, and a PhD in Computational Cognitive Neuroscience from Jain University, Bengaluru.

Dr. Kounte is a Senior Member of IEEE and a member of several international professional bodies, including IETE and ISTE. He has published over 20 indexed journal papers, 25+ international conference papers, 2 books, and 7 book chapters. His contributions have earned him 2 international patents, 1 design patent, and 6 Indian patents. His research work has garnered more than 500 citations in Scopus, with an h-index of 12.

He currently guides 5 PhD scholars and has successfully supervised 4 to completion. His research interests span Machine Learning, IoT Edge Computing, Internet of Vehicles, Signal Processing, Wireless Communication, and Blockchain Technologies. Dr. Kounte also heads the Machine Learning and Blockchain (MLB) research lab at REVA University and serves as a reviewer for various esteemed international journals, including IEEE, John Wiley, Springer, Elsevier, and MDPI.

Dr. Manjunath Kounte, Professor and Head of Electronics and Computer Engineering at REVA University, Bengaluru, has been a reviewer for this book. With an extensive background in Machine Learning, IoT Edge Computing, Blockchain Technologies, and more, his insights have contributed to refining the quality of this work.

Introduction

Introduction

- The Fundamentals of AI
- Evolution and Progression of AI Over Time
- Why Cybersecurity Matters in AI
- Overview of AI Threat Landscape

AI is a ground-breaking technology that mimics human intellect to accomplish various activities. Machine learning is a critical component of AI, allowing computers to learn from data and improve their performance over time. Deep learning is a subset of machine learning that uses neural networks to evaluate large quantities of data and produce accurate predictions or classifications. AI has practical applications in various fields, including banking and healthcare. AI systems can handle complicated problems, understand natural language, and detect patterns. With the ongoing progress of AI technology, the potential for innovation and revolution is enormous.

The Fundamentals of AI

AI, or artificial intelligence, emulates human intellect in computers to accomplish tasks. AI systems use techniques like machine learning to learn from data and enhance performance. Natural language processing (NLP) is an area of artificial intelligence that focuses on processing human language to communicate with machines. Other aspects of AI include computer vision, which analyses and comprehends visual data, and robotics, which blends AI with physical robots to do tasks autonomously. AI can do complex tasks previously exclusively performed by humans, making it a valuable tool in various sectors.

- **The Fundamentals of Machine Learning and Deep Learning:**

Machine learning, a kind of artificial intelligence, enables computers to learn from data without explicit programming. Supervised learning trains models using labeled data, whereas unsupervised learning identifies patterns in unlabeled data. Deep learning is a subset of machine learning using several layers of neural networks. Deep neural networks, including convolutional neural networks, are used in computer vision and speech recognition applications. The essence of machine learning is its capacity to allow computers to learn and improve from experience through data-driven techniques. Machine learning and deep learning have transformed the area of artificial intelligence by utilizing hidden layers and complicated algorithms, providing strong tools for analyzing and comprehending massive volumes of data.

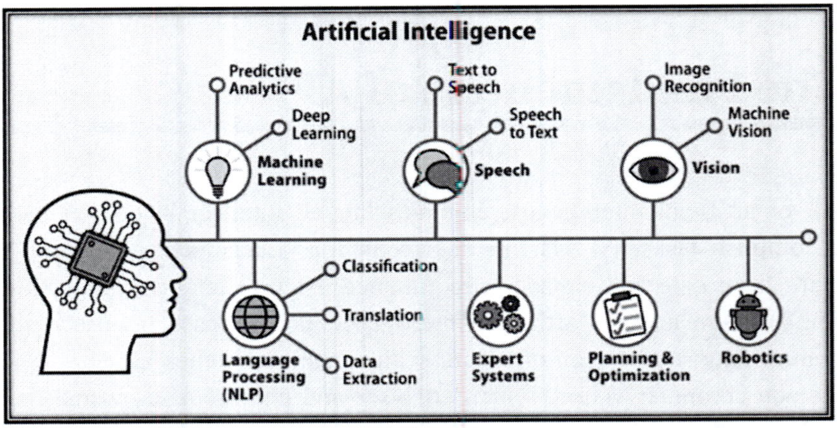

➢ Historical Development of AI

The discipline of artificial intelligence (AI) was founded in 1956, although its roots date back to the 1940s. Initially, AI systems were designed to solve specific tasks such as chess or math problems. In the 1950s and 1960s, expert systems were developed that used rules to simulate human competence. However, in the 1980s, AI faced issues, resulting in the "AI winter." Fortunately, the 21st century saw a rebirth in AI, mainly due to advances in processing power and extensive data. AI already has widespread applications in various areas, including healthcare and finance. The historical history of AI shows how it evolved from its inception to becoming a vital part of our lives.

➢ Birth and Early Years of AI

The origins of AI may be traced back to a 1956 meeting at Dartmouth College, where pioneers like Allen Newell, John McCarthy, and Marvin Minsky convened to investigate the possibility of artificial intelligence. Early AI systems, such as the Logic Theorist and General Problem Solver, revealed the power of AI in tackling complicated issues. The 1960s saw substantial advances in natural language processing and machine vision methods, which broadened the field of AI applications. However, in the 1970s, funding for AI research declined, slowing development. Nonetheless, the foundation created in the early years of AI cleared the path for further developments and set the stage for the creation of intelligent technology that we see today.

Evolution and Progression of AI Over Time

Over the years, AI has evolved and progressed significantly. During the 1980s and 1990s, there was a greater emphasis on expert systems and rule-based AI, which sought to duplicate human competence. The 2000s saw advancements in machine learning, neural networks, and extensive data processing, opening the path for increasingly powerful artificial intelligence applications. Recent advances in deep learning, natural language processing, and computer vision have catapulted AI to new heights, allowing for its incorporation into various fields, such as virtual assistants and self-driving cars. Ongoing research and breakthroughs continue to influence the future of AI technology, pushing its limits and paving the way for additional improvements. AI has sprung into the public in recent years with the emergence of simple tools that are already disrupting industries such as site design, copyrighting, and media creation. Many influential thought leaders, including rich celebrities like Elon Musk and Bill Gates, are now discussing AI. These improvements and widespread usage of tools have prompted several worries about AI's efficacy and influence on ordinary culture.

➢ Exploring Several Types of AI

AI technology is divided into two categories: strong AI and weak AI. Strong AI, often known as artificial general intelligence (AGI), refers to systems demonstrating human-like intelligence in various circumstances. In contrast, weak or limited AI is intended for specialized tasks such as speech recognition and picture classification. Reactive machines are a sort of weak AI that responds to inputs without memory or learning capabilities. Limited memory AI systems use data to improve performance but are job-specific.

Another frontier of AI research focuses on the Theory of Mind and self-awareness to understand human-like intelligence. These many forms of AI demonstrate artificial intelligence technology's broad capabilities, ranging from narrowly targeted applications to the possibility of human-like intellect. As more research is undertaken, we should expect even more significant improvements in AI applications in the healthcare, finance, and transportation industries. Robot Man

➢ Distinguishing Between Strong and Weak AI

Strong AI, commonly called artificial general intelligence, seeks to imitate human intellect, whereas weak AI is task-specific. Strong AI systems have broad intelligence and attempt to emulate human cognition, whereas weak AI systems focus on specialized tasks and employ techniques such as machine learning. Weak AI is now extensively used in various applications, but developing strong AI is a long-term objective. Strong and weak AI have potential advantages and drawbacks, necessitating ethical concerns. It is critical to distinguish between the two as we continue to investigate the potential and limitations of AI technology.

Why Cybersecurity Matters in AI

The importance of cybersecurity should not be underestimated. Organizations increasingly rely on gadgets and virtual systems as technology becomes more widely adopted.

Cybersecurity protects information, but it must grow. It must be updated to identify new threats and keep up with cybercriminals' evolving tactics. Cybersecurity frequently uses AI to monitor systems and discover problems before they escalate into more significant difficulties.

AI plays a vital role in cybersecurity by performing the following tasks:

- **Additional Protection:** AI examines data for anomalies. If abnormalities are discovered, specialists are notified so that they may address problems before they worsen. It decreases response time, allowing teams to respond rapidly.
- **Risk Management:** AI technology discovers flaws and dangers to assure system security. It may also provide event reports, allowing teams to identify the source of threats and respond appropriately. Statistics suggest that this increased research efficiency by 55%.
- **Balancing UX and Security**: While cybersecurity safeguards data, it may also make it harder for people to access it. AI makes the procedure more manageable by using facial and fingerprint recognition. It also assesses the risks associated with log-in attempts and detects phishing and malware

AI provides several benefits to enterprises, including:

- **Keeping Information Safe:** AI's capacity to improve system safety and discover dangers early on saves data, minimizes disruptions when systems fail, and protects the company's brand.
- **Scalability**: AI can scan and process enormous amounts of data as needed.
- **Learning and Adapting**: AI is constantly learning from the data it gets and evolving to meet the needs of new threats and systems.
- **Improving Efficiency**: By delegating threat detection to AI, teams may focus on more important responsibilities.

AI Technologies Used for Cybersecurity

Machine learning (ML) enables systems to learn without requiring extra programming. It employs User and Entity Behavior Analytics (UEBA) to examine cybersecurity-related trends and behaviors, detecting assaults early and mitigating them before they become significant problems.

Deep Learning: This subset of machine learning detects sophisticated threats using neural networks. It can identify polymorphic malware, malicious software that changes its code to avoid detection. Neural networks are AI models inspired by the human brain. Each node processes input data to refine accuracy. In cybersecurity, enormous amounts of data are analyzed to predict future threats.

- **Large Language Models (LLMs)** interpret threat reports and system logs and documentation. These technologies help to prevent phishing situations and respond faster.
- AI integration must be appropriately handled, taking into account all inherent hazards. To optimize the benefits of AI in cybersecurity, organizations can integrate procedures like:
- **Understanding Limitations:** While AI is an excellent danger prevention system, it learns mostly from internet data, which might include erroneous, incomplete, or biased data.

Furthermore, because it relies on existing data, it may fail to respond to new threats. Organizations must realize AI's limits and integrate human experience with AI to ensure seamless operations.

- **Ensuring Ethical and Transparent Integration:** Some various norms and regulations regulate cybersecurity. Organizations must guarantee that AI systems adhere to these standards, eliminate biases, and encourage openness in decision-making. Ethical norms must be observed to avoid compromising information.
- **Addressing Potential AI Attacks:** While AI safeguards systems, it may also introduce vulnerabilities. Criminals with expertise in AI can exploit the technology, causing it to miss or misunderstand threats. Such assaults will be prevented by rigorous testing, monitoring, and investment in defensive measures.
- **Investing in Trusted Systems:** Organizations may mitigate dangers by purchasing systems with sophisticated cybersecurity features such as safe data storage, encryption, and access restrictions. Regular audits guarantee that systems comply with current trends and compliance laws.
- **Ensuring Smooth Integration:** Not all AI systems interface seamlessly with current cybersecurity frameworks. Organizations should engage with professionals to determine the best solutions for their existing infrastructure and prevent costly processing power and infrastructure changes.

Overview of AI Threat Landscape

These days, the discourse around AI frequently focuses on its safety and ethical applications. What is commonly forgotten is the security and safety of the AI systems themselves. AI-based solutions, like any other technology, may be exploited by attackers, resulting in disruption, financial loss, reputational injury, or even risking human health and life.

There are three Main Types of AI Attacks:

➢ **Adversarial Machine Learning Attacks:**

These assaults try to modify AI systems' behavior, elude discovery, or steal the underlying technology.

➢ **Generative AI System Attacks:**

These assaults aim to generate dangerous or unlawful information by evading AI system filters and prohibitions.

➢ **Supply Chain Attacks:**

These attacks occur when a trusted third-party vendor is hacked, compromising the goods purchased from them.

- Understanding Adversarial Machine Learning Attacks requires familiarity with fundamental terms.
- Artificial intelligence is any system that resembles human intellect.
- Machine learning is the technique that allows AI to learn and improve its predictions.
- Machine Learning Models are the decision-making mechanisms that underpin most current artificial intelligence.
- Model training is entering data into a machine-learning algorithm, which results in a trained model.

Adversarial attacks on machine learning usually attempt to change the model's behavior, circumvent or escape the model, or reproduce the model or its data. These assaults include approaches such as data poisoning, which alters the model's behavior during training.

Data Poisoning attacks attempt to alter the model's behavior. To support their purpose, the attacker aims to make the forecasts biased, erroneous, or otherwise distorted. Attackers can use data poisoning in two ways: by changing existing dataset entries or inserting a new, intentionally doctored data section.

Model evasion, or model bypass, involves manipulating model inputs to create incorrect classifications. Adversaries repeatedly use forged queries to test the model's decision bounds. These attacks have been seen in various systems, including spam filters and intrusion detection systems.

Attacks on AI systems can also be motivated by intellectual property theft, often known as model theft. Adversaries may attempt to steal the model, rebuild training data, or produce nearly similar clones. These assaults threaten both intellectual property and data privacy.

Attacks Specific to Generative AI

Generative AI systems confront particular issues, such as prompt injection, which tricks AI bots into executing unwanted behaviors, and code injection, which permits unauthorized code execution.

Supply Chain Attacks

By exploiting trust and reach, these attacks impact downstream customers of hacked items. Vulnerabilities in model repositories, third-party contractors, and ML tools pose serious dangers in artificial intelligence.

Attacks on AI systems are already occurring, but their extent and breadth are challenging to determine owing to a lack of awareness and monitoring. Understanding these dangers is critical for creating comprehensive security measures to protect AI systems and reduce possible harm. As AI improves, proactive initiatives to address security threats must grow concurrently to enable responsible AI development and implementation.

These days, the discourse around AI frequently focuses on its safety and ethical applications. What is commonly forgotten is the security and safety of the AI systems themselves. AI-based solutions, like any other technology, may be exploited by attackers, resulting in disruption, financial loss, reputational injury, or even risking human health and life.

This chapter explores the fundamentals of artificial intelligence (AI), highlighting its evolution and advancement over time. It underscores the critical importance of cybersecurity within AI, emphasizing how increased reliance on AI systems has expanded vulnerabilities and threats. The chapter provides an overview of the current AI threat landscape, detailing various security risks and challenges posed by sophisticated cyber-attacks, and stresses the necessity for robust cybersecurity measures to protect AI-driven technologies.

Contents

Part - 1: Understanding AI and Cybersecurity

Chapter - 1
Cybersecurity 101 – The Digital Battlefield 2

Chapter - 2
Cloud-Based AI Security Challenges And Solutions 16

Chapter - 3
AI As A Double-Edged Sword 27

Chapter - 4
Fundamentals Of AI And Machine Learning 35

Part - 2: Major Cybersecurity Risks in AI

Chapter - 5
Data Poisoning Attacks 54

Chapter - 6
Adversarial Attacks On AI Models 66

Chapter - 7
AI-Powered Social Engineering & Deepfakes 79

Chapter - 8
AI Model Theft And Intellectual Property Risks 99

Chapter - 9
Privacy And Ethical Risks Of AI 109

Chapter - 10
Supply Chain Security For AI Systems 125

Chapter - 11
AI Security In Iot And Edge Computing Environments 135

Part - 3: Defending AI Systems from Cyber Threats

Chapter - 12
Secure AI Development And Deployment 146

Chapter - 13
AI Security Testing Methodologies. 156

Chapter - 14
AI Security Metrics And Benchmarking 169

Chapter - 15

Future-Proofing AI Against Cyber-Attacks 180

Conclusion 191

Part – 1: Understanding AI and Cybersecurity

Chapter - 1

Cybersecurity 101 – The Digital Battlefield

Chapter 1

Cybersecurity 101 – The Digital Battlefield

- Core principles of Cyber Security
- Types of Cyber Threats
- Cryptography for Data Protection

1.1 Core Principles of Cybersecurity

Cybersecurity is securing computer systems, networks, and digital data against unauthorized access, use, disclosure, interruption, alteration, or destruction. As technology has grown more intertwined in our daily lives, the demand for strong cybersecurity measures has increased. Cybersecurity entails applying several security measures, tactics, and best practices to protect information and avoid cyber threats such as hacking, data breaches, and malware assaults. It includes several principles and concepts to create a safe and resilient digital environment. Adhering to these principles allows organizations to successfully minimize risks, secure sensitive data, and maintain the integrity and availability of their digital assets. In this post, we will look at the four fundamental concepts of cybersecurity and their importance in protecting against cyber-attacks.

Cybersecurity Principles

Protect: This concept focuses on protecting systems and data against unauthorized access, alteration, or destruction. It entails implementing security measures like firewalls, access restrictions, and encryption to prevent security breaches and secure sensitive data. Organizations may lower the likelihood of successful attacks while maintaining the confidentiality and integrity of their data by implementing strong password rules and performing frequent security updates.

Monitoring is critical for detecting and responding to any suspicious or harmful behavior in networks. This approach entails using monitoring tools and strategies to identify cyber threats and intrusions. Organizations can detect and mitigate possible security problems by continually monitoring system logs, network traffic, and user behavior. Proactive monitoring can also assist in discovering risks and potential areas for development in the infrastructure.

Assess: Risk assessment and vulnerability management are fundamental aspects of cybersecurity. Organizations should do frequent vulnerability assessments on their systems, networks, and applications. This involves carrying out penetration tests, vulnerability scans, and risk assessments in order to detect weaknesses and prioritize security measures.

Understanding their risk profile allows organizations to make educated decisions and deploy resources more efficiently to solve the most pressing issues.

Respond: It is vital to have incident response strategies and processes in place in case of a cybersecurity occurrence. This approach entails creating a thorough incident response strategy, which includes standards for containment, eradication, and recovery. Prompt and coordinated reaction activities can reduce the effect of security events, restore regular operations, and prevent future attacks.

Principle 1:

Identify the Risks and Weaknesses

Cybersecurity aims to secure systems and data from unauthorized access and dangerous activity. To do this, numerous principles govern the creation and execution of good cybersecurity initiatives. One of these essential ideas is to identify risks and weaknesses. Identifying possible risks and vulnerabilities allows organizations to assess the amount of threat they face proactively and prioritize their security solutions accordingly. This technique entails doing risk assessments and vulnerability scans to identify flaws in systems, networks, and applications. Organizations may improve their security posture by identifying the risks and vulnerabilities they face.

1.2 Types of Threats

Types of Threats to Information Security

In today's linked world, protecting our digital information is critical. Various threats to information security exist, each with unique characteristics and possible consequences.

A typical attack is an advanced persistent threat (APT). APTs are sophisticated, long-term cyber-attacks that target specific organizations or individuals. They frequently use reconnaissance, meticulous planning, and covert penetration tactics to obtain unauthorized access to sensitive data.

Malware like viruses and worms may infect systems and cause harm. Viruses embed themselves in files or programs and propagate when they are executed. Worms do not require a host file to propagate and may multiply over computer networks.

Malware, which stands for malicious software, is a broad term comprising various destructive programs. These include spyware, adware, and ransomware. Spyware collects information without the user's knowledge, adware displays intrusive adverts, and ransomware encrypts data and demands a fee to decrypt it.

Phishing schemes are fraudulent efforts to steal personal information such as usernames, passwords, or credit card numbers by impersonating a legitimate company. These scams are usually carried out by email, but they can also be carried out over the phone or through texts.

Understanding the nature of these threats and their possible influence on information security is critical for establishing effective security solutions. By remaining attentive and using proper security measures, individuals and organizations may better defend themselves from these attacks.

Assessing Risk and Vulnerability

Assessing risk and exposure is a critical component of cybersecurity. Organizations may secure their data and resources more effectively by detecting and monitoring possible risks early in the system development life cycle (SDLC). This technique involves the following steps:

Identify hazards: The first step is identifying any possible information system hazards. This entails reviewing various elements, including system architecture, network infrastructure, user behavior, and external threats. Organizations can identify regions at risk of attacks or breaches by undertaking a thorough evaluation.

Measure Risks

Once hazards have been identified, the next stage is to assess their possible effect and likelihood. This may be accomplished by giving a numerical value to each risk based on characteristics such as the threat's intensity, probability of occurrence, and potential outcomes.

Organizations can better prioritize their efforts and allocate resources if they estimate the risks.

Locate vulnerabilities: After reviewing the risks, it is critical to identify any existing vulnerabilities in the system. Vulnerability scans, penetration testing, and code reviews uncover holes that cyber attackers may exploit. Keep an up-to-date list of vulnerabilities to guarantee prompt repair.

Fix Vulnerabilities: Once vulnerabilities have been found, organizations must take prompt steps to mitigate them. This might include deploying patches and updates, instituting security controls, or redesigning specific system components. Regular vulnerability management methods, such as continuing monitoring and testing, are required to guarantee that new vulnerabilities are quickly found and addressed.

Organizations can protect their technology, information, and systems against cyber-attacks by analyzing risk and vulnerability. Continuous monitoring, updating, and adaptation are necessary to handle developing risks successfully.

Strategies for Managing Risk and Vulnerability

Managing risk and vulnerability in cybersecurity is critical for protecting sensitive data and resources from possible attackers. Organizations may reduce the impact of cyber assaults and the chances of successful breaches by implementing adequate procedures. Here are some essential methods to consider:

Implement Layered Defense: A layered defense strategy entails installing several security measures at various stages of the system. This technique assures that if one security control fails, the other levels may still offer protection. It comprises safeguards like firewalls, intrusion detection systems, antivirus software, and encryption.

Regularly Update and Patch Systems: Keeping software, apps, and operating systems up to date is critical for mitigating vulnerabilities. Regular system updates guarantee that known vulnerabilities are fixed, lowering the likelihood of exploitation by attackers.

Educate and train employees: Human error is a significant source of security breaches. Regular cybersecurity awareness training helps staff understand the dangers and best practices for data protection. Topics covered in training should include spotting phishing attempts, setting secure passwords, and recognizing social engineering strategies.

Conduct regular vulnerability assessments to discover flaws and potential entry points for attackers. By scanning systems and networks ahead of time, organizations can prevent vulnerabilities from being exploited.

Create Incident Response Plans: A well-defined incident response plan is critical for successfully dealing with cyber threats. It explains the measures to follow in the event of a security incident, including processes for controlling the attack, determining the reason, and resuming regular operations.

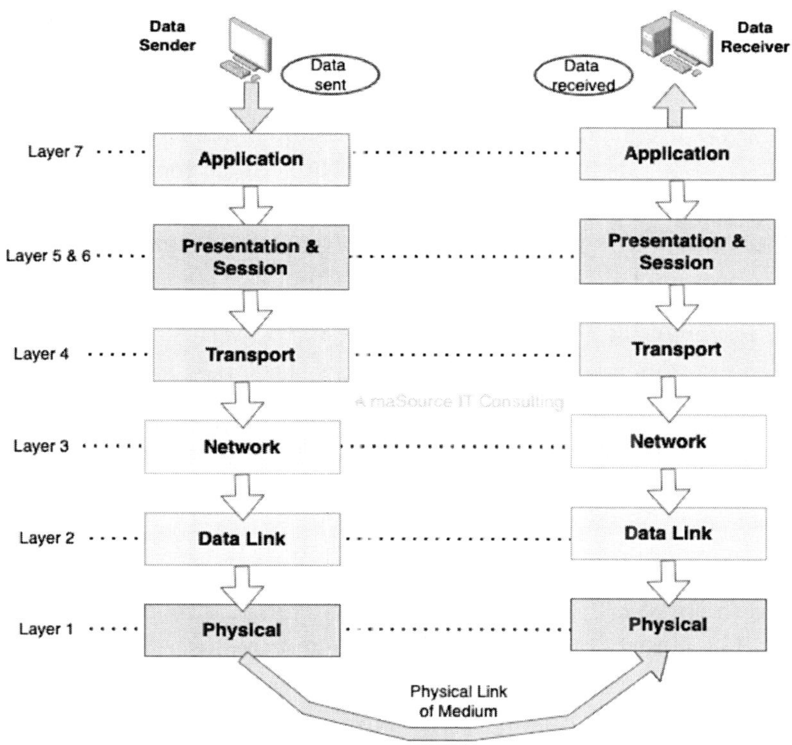

Principle 2:

Protect Data and Systems

Protecting data and systems is a core premise of cybersecurity. This concept emphasizes the need to secure sensitive information and the systems that store and handle it. Organizations may protect their data from unauthorized access, alteration, or loss by putting strong security measures in place. This idea encompasses critical measures, including encryption, access control, and backups. Data encryption guarantees that even if intercepted by unauthorized parties, it remains unreadable and unusable. Access control guarantees that only authorized users can access and alter data and systems. Regular data backups assist in defending against data loss caused by hardware failure, natural catastrophes, or malicious assaults. Securing data and systems is crucial for developing a strong cybersecurity posture and avoiding unauthorized access to sensitive information.

Access and Authorization Controls

Accessibility and authorization controls are essential ideas in cybersecurity that are critical for controlling user rights and guaranteeing the overall security of a system. These measures aim to prevent unauthorized access, reduce security risks, and safeguard sensitive data.

One essential idea is to provide consumers with minimum access privileges. Organizations can decrease the risk of misuse and unauthorized access to critical resources by allowing just the degree of access required to complete their jobs. This approach guarantees that users only have access to the information they need, reducing the potential harm in the event of a security breach.

Another key concept is the verification of user identities. Before allowing access to any user, verifying their identity using a strong authentication method is critical. This helps prevent unauthorized users from accessing the system, protecting critical information and resources.

Furthermore, it is critical to revoke access credentials once a task has been completed. Organizations may decrease the attack surface by withdrawing access privileges as soon as a user no longer needs them, ensuring that unauthorized persons cannot abuse lingering permissions.

1.3 Cryptography for Data Protection

Cryptography is critical for securing data and information from cyber threats. It entails using encryption methods and technology to turn plaintext data into ciphertext, rendering it inaccessible to unauthorized users.

Several encryption techniques are used to secure data. The most prevalent types are symmetric encryption, asymmetric encryption, and hashing. Symmetric encryption encrypt and decrypt data, whereas asymmetric encryption uses public and private keys for encryption and decryption, respectively. In contrast, hashing turns data into a fixed-length string of characters, making reverse engineering almost hard.

These methods use encryption technologies, enabling safe data transfer and storage. Secure Socket Layer (SSL) and Transport Layer Security (TLS) protocols are commonly used to encrypt data transported over the internet, whilst Virtual Private Networks (VPNs) allow for secure communication between remote sites.

Encryption is critical for data security because it secures information's secrecy, integrity, and validity. It protects sensitive data against unauthorized access, breaches, and theft. In the event of a security compromise, encrypted data is worthless to attackers without the decryption key. Furthermore, encryption enables organizations to comply with data protection rules while maintaining consumer confidence.

Backup, Recovery, and System Availability

Systems backup, recovery, and availability are critical parts of cybersecurity. These measures are essential for preventing data loss or harm in the event of a security breach.

Regular backups guarantee that copies of critical data are safely saved and recoverable in case of a data breach, accidental loss, or device failure. Backups are a safety net, enabling businesses to recover their systems and data quickly and effectively. It removes the danger of losing crucial information while reducing downtime.

Recovery techniques are equally vital. They detail the actions and processes for recovering systems and data, ensuring that activities can continue as soon as feasible. Organizations should develop comprehensive recovery programs that involve frequent testing to ensure their efficacy. These preparations ensure that data and systems can be recovered swiftly, avoiding long-term interruption and financial loss.

Redundancy, fault tolerance, and disaster recovery are all methods and procedures that organizations should employ to ensure the availability and accessibility of systems and data. Redundancy is the process of replicating key components, systems, or data to eliminate single-point failure. Fault tolerance guarantees that systems continue functioning even when a component or system fails. Disaster recovery plans include rules and methods for recovering operations following a significant calamity.

Offline backups are an extra fail-safe strategy for safeguarding vital data. Storing data offline keeps it safe from internet risks like ransomware assaults. Since hackers cannot exploit offline backups, they offer an additional layer of protection and peace of mind.

Principle 3:

Observe activity in networks, systems, applications, services, and data sources.

Effective cybersecurity necessitates ongoing attention and proactive monitoring of networks, systems, applications, services, and data sources. This approach requires the continual monitoring and analysis of events and activities inside an organization's infrastructure to discover any dangers or abnormalities. By regularly monitoring network traffic, system logs, and user behavior, cybersecurity experts may detect and respond to security events in real time. This approach also involves keeping track of external data sources and threat intelligence feeds to stay current on the newest cyber threats and vulnerabilities. Implementing strong monitoring systems and technologies enables businesses to identify and manage security breaches, unauthorized access attempts, and other harmful activities before they are substantial. Organizations may maintain a strong security posture and reduce the effect of cyber assaults by constantly monitoring their digital assets.

Network Security Monitoring

Network security monitoring is critical for protecting organizations from cyber threats and assaults. It entails continual tracking of network traffic to identify any evidence of unauthorized access or malicious behavior. Organizations that use efficient network security monitoring methods may proactively identify and respond to security events, reducing the harm caused by cyber assaults.

Network security monitoring assists in identifying and preventing cyber risks and assaults by giving real-time insight into network activity. It enables the discovery of aberrant behavior and the early detection of security breaches, allowing appropriate action to be performed. Security experts can discover and respond to possible security problems, such as unauthorized access, malware infections, or data exfiltration, by analyzing network logs, traffic patterns, and other network data.

To achieve effective network security monitoring, organizations need to adopt essential technologies and solutions, including Security

Information and Event Management (SIEM) and Security Operations Centres (SOC). SIEM gathers and analyses security events, logs, and data from many network sources in order to identify and investigate potential security breaches. SOC, on the other hand, is a centralized team tasked with monitoring network activity, investigating security incidents, and coordinating incident response efforts.

System Monitoring

System Monitoring: Reducing Security Incidents with Vigilance

System monitoring is crucial in cybersecurity because it helps organizations reduce security events by giving real-time visibility into their IT infrastructure. It entails continual monitoring of individual systems, user activity, and network traffic to detect any suspicious or aberrant behavior that might suggest a cybersecurity breach.

Individual system monitoring is an essential component of any complete monitoring plan. This includes monitoring system performance, resource utilization, and software vulnerabilities, as well as ensuring that relevant security patches and upgrades are implemented on a timely basis. Monitoring individual systems allows organizations to detect and resolve vulnerabilities before attackers exploit them proactively.

Another key part of system monitoring is tracking user actions. Monitoring user activity and access privileges assists in spotting any unauthorized or suspicious behavior that might signal a security compromise. This involves monitoring login attempts, user account activity, and access to sensitive data or vital systems. Organizations can avoid or minimize security issues by analyzing user activity to detect possible insider threats or unauthorized access attempts.

A good monitoring technique includes cleaning the monitoring data. With a rising amount of security logs and events being created, it is critical to filter and prioritize important warnings to focus on real security issues. By using intelligent monitoring and alerting solutions, organizations may decrease noise and false positives, allowing security personnel to focus on actual risks and respond promptly to security issues.

A critical component of system monitoring is examining and recording lessons acquired from prior security events. Organizations may enhance their security posture and prevent similar occurrences in the future by analyzing previous incidents to find vulnerabilities or gaps in their systems and procedures. This continuous learning and development methodology enables organizations to remain ahead of emerging threats while maintaining a strong cybersecurity posture.

Application Monitoring

Application monitoring is critical in cybersecurity because it enables organizations to detect and prevent flaws and intrusions in their apps and APIs. Organizations may assure the integrity and availability of their systems while also protecting against possible cybersecurity risks by continually monitoring application performance, behavior, and security.

Documentation is a vital component of application monitoring. This includes extensively documenting the application's design, architecture, and functioning, as well as any potential flaws or security issues. Organizations with detailed documentation can better understand and detect possible areas of vulnerability or sites of attack.

Approval is a crucial aspect of application monitoring. Before launching any application or API, organizations must verify that adequate security measures are followed and that all essential clearances are received. This involves doing security assessments, vulnerability scans, and code reviews to detect and correct any potential bugs or security issues.

Encoding is another crucial aspect of application monitoring. Organizations should ensure that apps and APIs have secure coding methods and frameworks. This helps prevent attackers from exploiting typical vulnerabilities, such as injection attacks and cross-site scripting.

Finally, monitoring strategies are essential in application monitoring. This entails implementing real-time monitoring tools to identify and notify organizations of any anomalous or suspicious behavior in their apps or APIs. By proactively monitoring for abnormalities, organizations may swiftly detect and respond to possible invasions or security breaches, lowering the risk of data loss or unauthorized access.

Service Monitoring

Service monitoring is a vital cybersecurity strategy that enables organizations to successfully secure their networks, systems, and data from possible attacks and breaches. Organizations may prevent big security problems by regularly monitoring the many parts of their services.

To successfully deploy service monitoring, organizations must first design a comprehensive monitoring plan. This includes defining the exact systems, applications, and networks that need to be monitored, as well as creating explicit monitoring goals and objectives. By concentrating on particular systems, organizations may acquire a more in-depth understanding of their vulnerabilities and dangers, allowing them to prioritize and reinforce their security measures accordingly.

User actions are also necessary for service monitoring. Organizations can discover odd or unauthorized acts that may suggest a security breach or an insider threat by monitoring user behavior and activity. This includes looking for suspicious login attempts, strange file access patterns, and unauthorized configuration modifications. Organizations may discover and respond to possible security problems by closely monitoring user activity.

Another critical component of service monitoring is cleaning the monitoring data. With the rising number of data created by diverse IT systems, organizations must simplify and centralize monitoring data. This may be accomplished by utilizing sophisticated analytics and visualization technologies that filter and show relevant information to security analysts, allowing them to detect and respond to possible risks more effectively.

Organizations should regularly examine and document the lessons learned from their monitoring operations. Organizations can detect repeating trends, security vulnerabilities, and opportunities for development by analyzing previous security events and monitoring data. This enables businesses to continually improve their monitoring methods and security measures in order to keep one step ahead of any cyber-attacks.

This chapter introduces the fundamental concepts of cybersecurity, emphasizing its critical role in the modern digital world. It starts by discussing the core principles of cybersecurity, which include the need for confidentiality, integrity, and availability of information. The chapter then explores the various types of cyber threats, ranging from malware and phishing to more sophisticated attacks, outlining the risks these pose to individuals and organizations. Finally, it delves into the importance of cryptography in securing data, explaining how encryption techniques help protect sensitive information from unauthorized access and ensure secure communication in digital environments.

Chapter - 2

Cloud-Based AI Security Challenges and Solutions

Chapter 2

Cloud-Based AI Security Challenges and Solutions

- ➢ Security Risks of Cloud-Based AI Systems
- ➢ AI-as-a-Service (AIaaS) Platforms
- ➢ Secure Deployment of AI Models in the Cloud
- ➢ Best Practices for Secure Deployments

2.1 Security Risks of Cloud-Based AI Systems

With scalable resources and enhanced capabilities, artificial intelligence (AI) systems that are hosted on the cloud have become an essential component in a variety of industries. On the other hand, the implementation of these systems brings about a wide range of security threats, which organizations need to address in order to protect sensitive data and preserve the integrity of their systems.

1. Data Breach

Data that is stored and processed on the cloud puts artificial intelligence systems at risk of being accessed by unauthorized parties. It is possible for attackers to get access to sensitive information by exploiting flaws in cloud infrastructure or artificial intelligence algorithms. This information may include training data, models, and user data. These kinds of breaches can result in severe financial losses as well as damage to a company's reputation. At the same time, as it is vital to implement stringent access restrictions, it is also essential to provide powerful encryption for data both while it is at rest and while it is in transit.

2. The Manipulation of Models

Threat actors have the ability to influence artificial intelligence models in order to generate biased or wrong outcomes, which can result in faulty forecasts or mistakes in decision-making. This may be accomplished through a variety of methods, including the introduction of malicious data into the training set or the exploitation of flaws in the architecture of the model being used. Regularly auditing artificial intelligence models and putting safe coding procedures into place can be helpful in detecting and preventing manipulations of this kind.

3. Denial of Service Attacks (also known as DoS)

When a denial of service assault (DoS) is launched against a cloud-based artificial intelligence system, the attackers flood the system with an overwhelming amount of traffic, making it inaccessible to those who are authorized to use it. These kinds of interruptions have the potential to halt essential activities and result in significant losses. Detecting and mitigating the effects of these assaults can be facilitated by the use of network security measures such as firewalls and intrusion detection systems.

4. Infections Caused by Malware

The integrity and performance of cloud systems can be compromised when malware infects them and spreads using artificial intelligence algorithms. These infections have the potential to result in unauthorized data access, contamination of models, and faults in the system. Implementing adequate endpoint security, doing vulnerability assessments on a regular basis, and updating software on a regular basis are all essential aspects in the prevention of computer malware attacks.

5. Dangers from Within

Those who are authorized to access cloud-based artificial intelligence systems have the potential to abuse their privileges in order to steal data or change models. Threats that originate from within an organization are notoriously tricky to identify and can have devastating effects. The implementation of robust authentication systems, the enforcement of access limits with the least amount of power, and the monitoring of user activity are all potential ways to assist in reducing these risks.

6. Attacks from our Adversaries

Attackers have the ability to build inputs that are intended to trick AI models, which can result in inaccurate outputs. These hostile attacks have the potential to compromise the dependability of artificial intelligence systems, particularly in crucial areas like healthcare and finance. Increasing the resilience of models may be accomplished by including adversarial training and performing frequent testing against known attack vectors, respectively.

7. The Poisoning of Data

In the context of data poisoning attacks, harmful data is injected into the training set, which results in learning processes that are warped and outputs that are unlikely to be dependable. The implementation of stringent data validation procedures and the elimination of suspect data inputs are both necessary steps in the prevention of assaults of this nature.

8. Breach of Confidentiality

Inadequate protection can result in privacy leaks caused by artificial intelligence systems, which frequently deal with sensitive information. The implementation of access restrictions, the encryption of data, and compliance with data protection legislation are all essential components in the process of protecting user privacy.

9. The Hijacking of Models and the Risks of Deployment

If a computer system that uses artificial intelligence is breached, the attackers can change the model or the infrastructure that it operates on, which might result in choices that are detrimental. The deployment of models within secure containers or virtual machines, as well as the implementation of access control measures, are both essential forms of protection against such risk.

10. Misuse of the API

APIs are frequently used to access cloud-based artificial intelligence models, which leaves them open to the possibility of unauthorized access as well as other security problems. When it comes to preventing misuse, putting in place robust authentication measures and monitoring API usage might be helpful.

Strategies for Risk Reduction

- In order for organizations to effectively handle these security problems, they need to adopt a holistic strategy that includes the following:

- Protecting the confidentiality of sensitive information requires encrypting it and putting in place access controls to stop unauthorized access.
- Adversarial Training: Increase the robustness of the model by integrating adversarial samples at various points throughout the training process.
- Continuous Monitoring and Auditing: Keep an eye out for any strange behavior shown by AI systems, and make sure to do security audits on a regular basis.
- Data Validation and Filtering: In order to prevent data poisoning, there should be systems in place to filter out data inputs that appear to be questionable.

- ➢ It is possible to restrict access to artificial intelligence models and infrastructure by using a system called role-based access control (RBAC).
- ➢ Ensuring that the underlying cloud infrastructure is safe, up-to-date, and set in accordance with industry standards is an important step.

It is possible for businesses to improve the security of their cloud-based artificial intelligence systems by putting these steps into effect. This will safeguard the systems from a wide variety of threats and ensure that they continue to function reliably.

2.2 AI-as-a-Service (AIaaS) Platforms

AI as a Service (AIaaS) is the delivery of artificial intelligence (AI) capabilities via cloud-based platforms on a subscription or pay-as-you-go model. Just as Software as a Service (SaaS) allows organizations to access software programs over the internet without owning the underlying infrastructure, AIaaS will enable businesses to harness AI technology without requiring in-house knowledge or hardware.

AIaaS includes a diverse set of AI tools and services, such as machine learning (ML), natural language processing (NLP), computer vision, and data analysis. Predictive analytics, customer support automation, personalized suggestions, and other duties may all be carried out using these technologies. AIaaS vendors provide ready-to-use APIs, development environments, and pre-trained models that can be seamlessly integrated into current systems, bringing AI to enterprises of all sizes. Despite its numerous advantages, AI as a Service faces significant problems that might jeopardize its efficacy and acceptance. One of the most pressing concerns is data privacy and security. When utilizing AIaaS, businesses must frequently provide sensitive data to third-party service providers, which might result in data breaches or misuse. Ensuring data security and compliance with legislation such as GDPR is critical for preserving trust and protecting consumer information.

Another key difficulty is a lack of control over the AI models and reliance on the service provider. Companies employing AIaaS may be restricted by the options and capabilities provided by their supplier. This might cause challenges with customization and flexibility since firms may be unable to design AI services to their individual needs fully. Additionally, there is the potential for vendor lock-in, which makes transferring to another supplier difficult and costly.

Finally, the quality of AIaaS is heavily reliant on the quality of the data given by users. Poor data quality can result in faulty models and unreliable outputs, reducing the usefulness of AI applications. Ensuring that data is reliable, comprehensive, and adequately organized is critical for getting the best results from AIaaS solutions. For additional information on these problems, check publications and resources on reliable websites such as TechCrunch or Harvard Business Review. Consider learning more about AI-as-a-Service (AIaaS) | Artificial Intelligence.

Data Privacy and Security

Data privacy and security are critical in the digital age, as data breaches and cyber-attacks are becoming more regular. As organizations and consumers rely more on digital platforms, the protection of sensitive information becomes increasingly important. Data privacy refers to people's ability to regulate how their personal information is gathered and utilized. Security, on the other hand, refers to the means and strategies used to keep this data safe against unauthorized access, theft, or damage.

One of the most pressing issues is how third-party vendors, such as cloud service providers and other technology companies, handle data. Companies must comply with worldwide data protection standards, such as the General Data Protection Regulation (GDPR) in Europe and the California Consumer Privacy Act (CCPA) in the United States. These rules establish tight data processing norms and give individuals great control over their personal information. GDPR.EU provides more thorough information about GDPR.

Furthermore, implementing strong cybersecurity safeguards is critical to maintaining data integrity and confidentiality. This involves using encryption, safe access procedures, and conducting regular security assessments. Organizations can also benefit from cybersecurity frameworks and standards like ISO/IEC 27001, which specifies the criteria for an information security management system (ISMS). More information about ISO/IEC 27001 may be obtained on the ISO website, ISO.org.

To summarise, ensuring data privacy and security is essential more than simply complying with the law; it is also about creating consumer trust and defending business reputation. Failure to safeguard data can result in significant financial losses and brand harm.

Quality of Service

Quality of Service (QoS) is essential in the performance and dependability of internet services and networks. QoS refers to a telecommunications service's overall performance from the perspective of the user, notably its predictability and consistency. This can include things like bandwidth, latency, error rates, and uptime. Ensuring good QoS is critical for organizations that rely on real-time data transmissions, such as video streaming, online gaming, and VoIP (Voice over IP).

Service providers employ a variety of methods to manage and improve QoS. These include traffic shaping, which prioritizes specific types of data, and Quality of Service protocols such as MPLS (Multi-Protocol Label Switching), which improve data flow efficiency across networks.

Cisco offers a complete guide to understanding how MPLS works, which can be found on Cisco.com.

Furthermore, adopting next-generation networking technologies like 5G and improved Wi-Fi standards can improve QoS by lowering latency and improving data transfer speeds. These technologies are critical to developing the Internet of Things (IoT) and other applications that demand dependable and immediate data sharing.

Businesses must constantly analyze and adjust their network performance to maintain high QoS. This includes annual infrastructure evaluations and updates, adapting to increased user needs, and new technology breakthroughs. Failure to maintain an acceptable degree of QoS can result in customer discontent, decreased productivity, and financial losses.

2.3 Secure Deployment of AI Models in the Cloud

The incorporation of generative AI models into commercial processes has opened up new avenues for automation, innovation, and decision-making. However, installing these sophisticated models securely on cloud platforms is critical for maintaining data integrity, compliance, and operational dependability. Organizations may maximize the benefits of AI while reducing risks by utilizing generative AI solutions, generative AI development services, and cloud security best practices.

Understanding Generative AI Models and their Applications

Generative AI models, such as GPT (Generative Pre-trained Transformer) and GANs (Generative Adversarial Networks), are intended to generate new material, such as text, photos, videos, and software code, using patterns learned from existing data. These models are increasingly being utilized in areas like healthcare, marketing, e-commerce, and entertainment to create content, personalize customers, innovate healthcare, and design and creativity. To properly deploy these models, enterprises frequently rely on generative AI development services, which offer expertise in AI system design, training, and security.

Advantages of Cloud-Based Deployment in Generative AI

Cloud platforms such as AWS, Google Cloud, and Microsoft Azure provide a stable infrastructure for implementing generative AI models, as well as scalability, cost-effectiveness, collaboration, and integration benefits. These platforms enable organizations to meet the computing needs of huge AI models while lowering initial costs and allowing for easy interaction with other cloud-based applications. However, putting generative AI models on the cloud creates new security problems that must be addressed.

Security Issues for Generative AI Deployment

Deploying generative AI models on cloud platforms poses a number of security risks, including data breaches, model theft, compliance problems, adversarial assaults, and internal threats. Unauthorized access to sensitive training data can cause data breaches, and model theft can result in severe intellectual property losses. Compliance with legislation such as GDPR and HIPAA is crucial, particularly in the healthcare and banking sectors. Adversarial attacks, in which bad actors influence AI models, and insider threats from workers or contractors exacerbate the security situation.

2.4 Best Practices for Secure Deployments

Addressing these issues necessitates a multifaceted strategy that blends cloud security standard practices with AI-specific measures. Data security techniques such as encryption, access restrictions, and data anonymization are critical for protecting sensitive information. Model protection includes intellectual property measures, API security, and federated learning to avoid theft and unauthorized use. Firewall configuration, logging, monitoring, and patch management all help to provide a secure cloud architecture. Adversarial defense methods, such as training models to detect malicious inputs, and compliance measures, such as frequent audits and adherence to industry norms, are also required.

The Role of Cloud Providers in Securing AI Deployments

Leading cloud providers provide capabilities and services that enable secure AI implementations. AWS offers Sage Maker for safe AI model training and deployment, as well as AWS KMS for reliable encryption. Google Cloud provides Vertex AI with built-in security controls and Assured Workloads for compliance. Microsoft Azure's Azure AI platform contains comprehensive security measures, including Azure Sentinel, which detects and responds to attacks. These solutions allow organizations to safely deploy generative AI models while taking advantage of cloud platforms' scalability and flexibility.

Enhancing Security through Generative AI Development Services

Generative AI development services improve security by providing bespoke AI model creation, safe deployment, continuous monitoring, and compliance support. These services guarantee that AI systems are created with security as a top priority and deployed in best-in-class environments. For example, a worldwide e-commerce business successfully implemented a generative AI-powered recommendation engine on a cloud platform by collaborating with a supplier of generative AI development services, assuring data protection, model integrity, and regulatory compliance.

Future Trends for Secure AI Deployment

Future developments in secure AI deployment include the use of zero-trust architectures, which remove implicit trust from cloud settings, as well as the use of AI-powered security technologies to identify and respond to attacks in real time. Decentralized AI models, developed and deployed on edge devices, improve security by limiting data exposure. Blockchain integration is also developing as a means of enhancing transparency and integrity in AI model deployment.

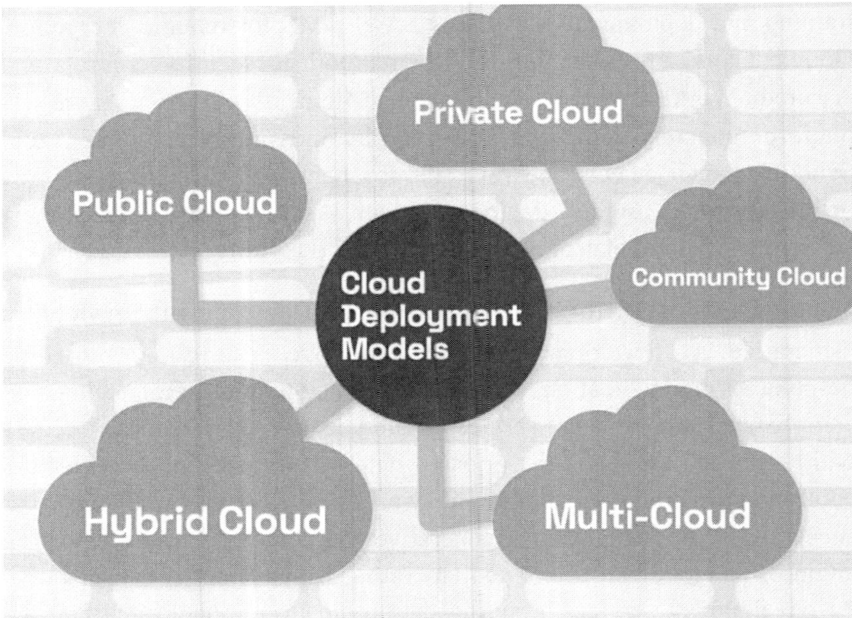

This chapter discusses the security challenges associated with cloud-based AI systems and outlines strategies for mitigating risks. It begins by identifying the security risks inherent in cloud-based AI, including data breaches, unauthorized access, and potential vulnerabilities due to the shared nature of cloud environments. The chapter also examines AI-as-a-Service (AIaaS) platforms, where AI solutions are delivered over the cloud, highlighting specific security concerns such as data privacy and the need for effective access control.

Chapter - 3
AI as a Double-Edged Sword

Chapter 3: AI as a Double-Edged Sword

- How AI Enhances Cybersecurity
- How AI Can Be Exploited by Cybercriminals

3.1 How AI Enhances Cybersecurity

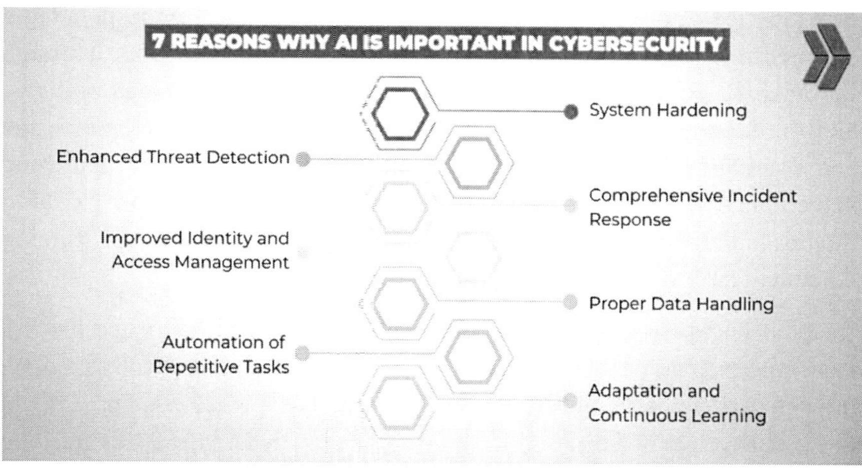

1. Assisted Detection and Response of Advanced Threats

Artificial intelligence is particularly adept at recognizing trends and abnormalities that may point to the presence of a cyber threat. Artificial intelligence (AI) systems utilize machine learning algorithms to analyze massive volumes of data and find unexpected behaviors that might imply an unknown danger. This is in contrast to traditional security systems, which depend on signature-based detection, which can only identify known threats. The ability to recognize zero-day vulnerabilities and advanced persistent threats (APTs), which frequently circumvent traditional detection methods, is of the utmost importance.

For instance, threat detection solutions that are powered by artificial intelligence are able to examine network traffic, user behavior, and even threat intelligence from the outside world in order to identify indications of an ongoing assault. The amount of time it takes to recognize and respond to threats is significantly cut down because of the capabilities of these tools, which allow them to function at a pace and scale that would be unthinkable for human analysts. Artificial intelligence also has the ability to rank these risks according to the potential damage they may do, which enables security personnel to concentrate their efforts on the most serious situations first.

2. Phishing Detection and Incident Response Systems That Are Fully Automated

The practice of phishing continues to be one of the most widespread and successful tactics that hackers use to attack computing systems. Through the analysis of email content, the identification of suspicious patterns, and the identification of possible phishing efforts before they reach the end user, artificial intelligence has the potential to improve phishing detection. Artificial intelligence (AI) systems can adapt to new phishing methods and increase their detection accuracy over time by utilizing machine learning.

Incident response is another area in which artificial intelligence plays a key role. Artificial intelligence systems can automatically isolate impacted systems, activate established response processes, and inform the security team if a possible danger is identified. All of this may be accomplished in seconds. Not only does this skill of fast reaction lessen the detrimental effects of the threat, but it also lessens the amount of work that security teams have to do, which enables them to concentrate on more strategic obligations.

3. Enhancing the Managed Detection and Response (MDR) capabilities existing inside Security Operations Centers (SOCs)

As businesses strive to improve their cybersecurity posture, Managed Detection and Response (MDR) services have become an increasingly significant component of their operational strategies. Artificial intelligence (AI) and machine learning technologies are revolutionizing the operation of security operations centers (SOCs), which are responsible for delivering real-time threat identification, automated analysis, and a more rapid reaction to incidents.

Using artificial intelligence, security operations centers (SOCs) are able to enhance their threat-hunting skills, recognize new threats, and deliver intelligence that is more precise and actionable. Data from various sources may be analyzed using MDR tools powered by artificial intelligence, which can then correlate the data with known threat indicators and even forecast future attack pathways. This increases the SOC's capacity to respond to threats in a timely manner and improves the overall security posture by lowering the time and effort necessary to handle and investigate events.

4. Using Predictive Analytics to Provide a Proactive Defense

AI makes it possible to take a preventative approach to cybersecurity through predictive analytics. Artificial intelligence can forecast possible attack vectors by analyzing past data and recognizing patterns. This enables organizations to build their defenses better in response to prospective threats. This talent is instrumental in figuring out potential dangers and taking preventative measures against them before they can cause any harm.

Additionally, predictive analytics powered by artificial intelligence may assist organizations in predicting future risks by utilizing current patterns and threat knowledge. For example, artificial intelligence systems may discover new tactics, methods, and procedures (TMPs) employed by cybercriminals by analyzing global threat data. These systems can then advise preventative steps to counteract these threats.

5. **Increasing the Robustness of Fraud Prevention and User Access Control**

User access control may be improved with the use of artificial intelligence by analyzing user behavior and locating anomalies that may indicate unauthorized access or access. An example of this would be how artificial intelligence models can evaluate the danger of each login attempt based on the expected behavior of the user and highlight behaviors that are questionable. This technique increases security and enhances user experience by eliminating the need for confirmed users to change their passwords frequently or to employ multi-factor authentication.

Additionally, artificial intelligence plays a significant role in fraud prevention by continuously analyzing transaction patterns and identifying fraudulent activity in real-time. An artificial intelligence system can assist in minimizing financial losses and safeguarding sensitive data from being exploited by recognizing and stopping suspicious transactions.

3.2 How AI Can Be Exploited by Cybercriminals

Cybercriminals use AI to carry out a variety of cyber assaults, including password cracking, phishing emails, impersonation, and deepfakes. It's critical that you understand how cybercriminals use AI to their advantage so you can better safeguard yourself, your family, and your accounts and data.

Here are a few ways thieves are using AI to execute cyber assaults

➢ AI Password Cracking

Password cracking is a method used by cybercriminals to get passwords. Cybercriminals frequently utilize password-cracking programs that exploit variants of widely used passwords or dictionary terms, attempting every conceivable combination until they successfully crack a password. This is often referred to as a brute force attack.

Home Security Heroes published a paper revealing that AI can quickly guess widely used passwords. This poses a significant security risk to users who do not utilize strong passwords on their accounts. The paper tested an AI-powered password-cracking tool, PassGAN, on over 15 million regularly used passwords. The study discovered that 51% of regularly used passwords can be cracked in less than a minute, 65% in an hour, 71% in a day, and 81% in a month.

➢ Artificial Intelligence-generated Phishing Emails

Phishing is a sort of social engineering assault that seeks to deceive the intended victim into disclosing sensitive information. Phishing emails used to be easy to detect because they had many grammatical and spelling errors, but AI is now making it simple for hackers to create well-written, convincing content for phishing schemes. Instead of creating their own phishing emails or text messages, fraudsters are using artificial intelligence to develop hoaxes for them. For example, artificial intelligence-generated phishing emails can replicate the tone, grammar, and style of authentic emails. This makes the hoax more plausible. Cybercriminals can also use AI to personalize emails based on data gathered from the internet or information fed to it.

➢ Artificial Intelligence Impersonation

When cybercriminals conduct phishing schemes, AI impersonation has grown more widespread. Vishing is a sort of phishing fraud that occurs over the phone. To carry out a vishing attack, a cybercriminal phones their target and claims to be someone they know, such as a coworker, acquaintance, or family member.

AI systems may generate a synthetic persona by analyzing enormous volumes of data. A cybercriminal can use artificial intelligence to impersonate someone's voice using a process known as synthesis. It accomplishes this by examining a person's voice from audio and video records and then producing speech that sounds exactly like the person it is imitating.

- **These phishing attacks are becoming more widespread as AI advances.**

Deepfakes are AI-generated material that alters a person's face or physique to make them appear different from them. They are frequently used maliciously to disseminate misleading information. Although deepfakes have been around for a while, they are becoming increasingly difficult to detect as technology progresses. Even law enforcement personnel are failing to recognize deepfakes.

Here are some strategies for avoiding AI-enabled cyber threats

Safeguard your accounts:

To prevent your data from being hacked, you should have robust account security in place. This includes using strong, unique passwords and enabling Multi-Factor Authentication (MFA) wherever permitted.

Strong passwords should never be repeated, be at least 16 characters long, include both capital and lowercase letters, and include digits and symbols. Creating and managing strong passwords might be difficult, but a password manager can help.

Password managers are applications that help users generate, manage, and securely save passwords. The finest password organizers can also keep track of your passkeys. The only password you'll need to remember is your master password, which serves as a key to unlock your vault.

Multi-factor authentication provides an additional degree of protection for your accounts. When MFA is enabled, users cannot successfully log in to their account without validating their identity using a preferred verification method, such as an authenticator app.

➢ Avoid Responding to Solicitations for Personal Information

Phishing schemes are designed to trick you into disclosing personal information, which hackers can then exploit to gain access to your accounts or steal your money. Because phishing schemes can occur by email, phone calls, or text messages, you must always exercise caution when sharing personal information.

For example, if you receive an email claiming to be from your bank and requesting sensitive information such as your card number, don't be too ready to believe it. Most businesses will not contact you unexpectedly and request personal information. Before responding to a request for personal information, contact the company or individual directly to ensure it is legitimate. When calling a firm, make sure you obtain their phone number from their official website.

➢ Avoid Clicking on Unsolicited Links or Attachments

Typical phishing schemes will also attempt to get you to click on dangerous links or files. If you get unsolicited links and attachments, you should avoid clicking on them. Clicking on them may result in a malware infection that puts all of your sensitive data at risk of compromise.

➢ Backup your Files on a Regular Basis

Any data on your devices should constantly be backed up. This is not simply a cybersecurity-recommended practice; it also protects your data if your device is stolen, lost, or broken. If your device is infected with malware, it would also prevent you from losing your data permanently.

We recommend that you save your data using an encrypted service. Some password managers may store information other than passwords. Keeper Password Manager, for example, has a Secure File Storage add-on that preserves many sorts of data, such as files and photos. All of the data saved here is encrypted and only accessible to the user. Please back up your data on a regular basis with a service like Secure File Storage to keep it out of the wrong hands.

➢ Keep your Software and Gadgets up to Date

Another cybersecurity best practice you should adopt is to update your software and devices as soon as a new version becomes available. Not only do updates include new functionality, but they also fix security flaws and vulnerabilities that may be exploited if not patched. Cybercriminals frequently seek out these vulnerabilities and manipulate them to target unsuspecting victims effectively.

- **Create a Safe Word for your Family**

Due to the rise of AI phishing schemes, developing a safe word with your family is suggested. Some of these scams have targeted older generations, convincing them that the person phoning is their grandchild. They frequently employ scenarios such as getting involved in a vehicle accident or being in jail and need money. If you establish a safe word with your family, you will know quickly if the person phoning is a family member needing assistance or a fraudster.

This chapter explores the dual nature of AI in the context of cybersecurity, presenting both the positive and negative impacts AI can have. It begins by highlighting how AI enhances cybersecurity, including its ability to quickly analyze large amounts of data to detect anomalies, improve threat detection, and automate responses to security breaches. AI-powered systems can also help predict future attacks by identifying patterns and potential vulnerabilities, improving overall defense strategies.

On the flip side, the chapter also discusses how AI can be exploited by cybercriminals. Malicious actors can use AI to develop more sophisticated attacks, such as advanced phishing schemes, AI-driven malware, and automated hacking tools. The ability of AI to learn and adapt makes it a potent tool for cybercriminals, posing significant challenges to traditional security measures.

Chapter - 4
Fundamentals of AI And Machine Learning

Chapter 4: Fundamentals of AI and Machine Learning

- How Deep Learning Works
- AI's Role in Critical Industries
- AI Processes and Analyzes Data

Artificial intelligence

The term "artificial intelligence" (AI) refers to the application of technologies to construct machines and computers capable of imitating cognitive functions associated with human intelligence. These functions include the ability to see, understand, respond to spoken or written language, analyze data, and make recommendations, among other things.

AI is a technology set that enables a system to reason, learn, and act to solve complicated issues. Although it is commonly thought of as a system in and of itself, artificial intelligence is a combination of technologies.

Machine Learning (ML)

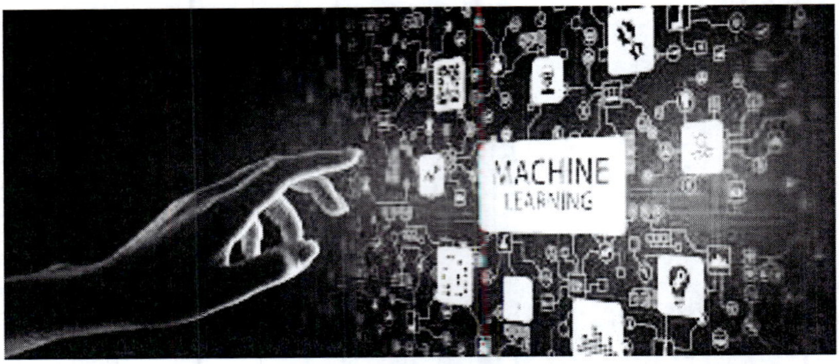

The goal of machine learning (ML), a subset of artificial intelligence (AI), is to automatically enable a computer or system to learn and grow from experience. In machine learning, rather than explicit programming, algorithms are used to analyze enormous volumes of data, aiming to learn from the insights gained and make decisions based on that learning. The performance of machine learning algorithms improves over time as they are taught with additional data, ultimately resulting in more accurate models.

Although AI and ML are closely related, they are not the same thing. While artificial intelligence (AI) refers to the more general notion of enabling a computer or system to detect, reason, act, or adapt like a person, machine learning (ML) refers to the ability of machines to extract information from data and learn on their own. Artificial intelligence (AI) is a catch-all phrase encompassing various methodologies and techniques, such as machine learning (ML), deep learning, robots, expert systems, and natural language processing.

The primary distinction between artificial intelligence (AI) and machine learning is found in their applications and aims. AI aims to create intelligent systems capable of executing complex tasks by imitating humans. On the other hand, machine learning is centered on instructing machines to carry out specific tasks and provide precise outcomes by recognizing patterns.

Example: When a user asks a Google Nest device, "How long is my commute today?" the gadget responds with the answer. Thanks to artificial intelligence, the gadget comprehends and reacts to the inquiry. At the same time, machine learning algorithms analyze real-time transit and traffic data to anticipate traffic flow and deliver an accurate estimate. AI guarantees that the system can do the task, while machine learning ensures that the system continuously learns and improves depending on the given data.

Through logic and decision-making processes, artificial intelligence enables robots to replicate human intellect to solve issues, construct intelligent systems for strenuous activities, and use a variety of data kinds. Machine learning, on the other hand, is a technique that enables computers to learn on their own from previous data, construct predictive models, and provide correct results within a specific range of applications by making use of structured and semi-structured data.

When combined, artificial intelligence and machine learning provide tremendous benefits to organizations by automating activities, unlocking revenue, and producing insights that can be implemented. As the volume and complexity of data increase, intelligent systems powered by artificial intelligence and machine learning become increasingly important for obtaining better results and fostering innovation across all industries.

Deep Learning

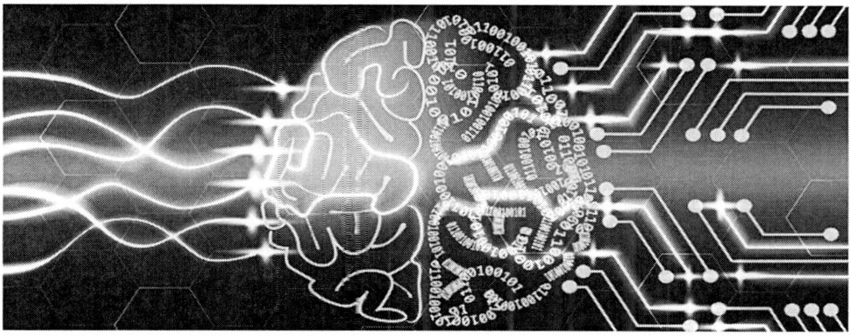

Deep learning is a subclass of machine learning that uses multilayered neural networks, or deep neural networks, to imitate the sophisticated decision-making capacity of the human brain. Most artificial intelligence (AI) apps we use today are powered by deep learning.

The primary distinction between deep and machine learning is the topology of the underlying neural network architecture. Traditional machine learning models, known as "nondeep," employ essential neural networks with one or two processing layers. Deep learning models train with three or more layers—typically hundreds or thousands.

While supervised learning models rely on structured, labeled input data to provide reliable results, deep learning models can employ unsupervised learning. Deep learning models can use unsupervised learning to extract the traits, features, and correlations required to provide correct results from raw, unstructured data. Furthermore, these models can analyze and update their results for greater accuracy.

Deep learning is a branch of data science that powers several applications and services that increase automation by executing analytical and physical activities without human interaction. This allows many everyday goods and services, like digital assistants, voice-enabled TV remotes, credit card fraud detection, self-driving vehicles, and generative AI.

4.1 How Deep Learning Works

Neural networks, or artificial neural networks, try to emulate the human brain by combining data inputs, weights, and biases that behave like silicon neurons. These components work together to identify, categorize, and characterize objects in data effectively.

Deep neural networks comprise numerous layers of linked nodes, with each layer refining and optimizing the preceding layer's prediction or categorization. Forward propagation refers to the flow of calculations over a network. A deep neural network's input and output layers are called "visible layers." The input layer is where the deep learning model receives data for processing, whereas the output layer is where the final prediction or classification is formed.

Backpropagation is a procedure that employs algorithms like gradient descent to compute errors in predictions before adjusting the function's weights and biases by going backward through the layers to train the model. Forward propagation and backpropagation allow a neural network to create predictions while correcting for mistakes. Over time, the algorithm improves in accuracy.

Deep learning needs a significant amount of computational power. High-performance graphics processing units (GPUs) are suitable since they can manage large operations over numerous cores while having enough memory. Distributed cloud computing may also help. This processing power is required to train deep algorithms using deep learning. However, managing numerous GPUs on-premises may significantly strain internal resources and be extremely expensive to grow. For software needs, most deep learning programs are written in one of three learning frameworks: JAX, PyTorch, or TensorFlow.

Types of Deep Learning Models

Deep learning algorithms are highly sophisticated, and several types of neural networks are designed to solve specific issues or datasets. Here are six. Each has its own set of benefits, shown below in a sequence of development, with each consecutive model modifying to compensate for a weakness in the prior model.

One possible flaw is that deep learning models are frequently "black boxes," making it difficult to grasp their inner workings and raising interpretability issues. However, this may be weighed against the overall advantages of high precision and scalability.

CNNs:

Convolutional neural networks (CNNs or ConvNets) are widely utilized in computer vision and image categorization applications. They can recognize characteristics and patterns in pictures and videos, allowing for tasks like object detection, image recognition, pattern recognition, and face recognition. These networks use linear algebra concepts, namely matrix multiplication, to find image patterns.

CNNs are a neural network comprised of node layers, including an input layer, one or more hidden layers, and an output layer. Each node connects to another and has a weight and threshold. If the output of any particular node exceeds the defined threshold value, that node is activated and sends data to the next tier of the network. Otherwise, no data is sent to the next tier of the network.

A CNN consists of at least three layers: convolutional, pooling, and fully connected (FC). A CNN might have thousands of layers for sophisticated applications, each building on the preceding levels. Detailed patterns can be identified by "convolution"—working and reworking the initial data. The CNN's complexity rises with each layer, allowing it to detect larger sections of the picture. Earlier layers concentrate on simple elements like colors and borders. As visual input goes through the CNN's layers, it begins to recognize more prominent components or features of the item, eventually identifying the target object.

CNNs are distinguished from other neural networks by their superior performance on image, speech, and audio signal inputs. Before CNNs, objects in pictures were identified manually and slowly using feature extraction methods. However, CNNs now provide a more scalable method for picture classification, object identification applications, and the ability to analyze high-dimensional data. Additionally, CNNs may share data between layers, resulting in more efficient processing. While information may be lost in the pooling layer, this may be compensated for by the benefits of CNNs, which can assist in decreasing complexity, enhancing efficiency, and lowering the danger of overfitting.

Other downsides of CNNs include their computing demands, which cost time and money and require using many graphics processing units. They also demand highly skilled professionals with cross-domain knowledge and rigorous testing of settings, hyperparameters, and configurations.

RNNs:

Recurrent neural networks (RNNs) are commonly utilized in natural language and voice recognition applications because they process sequential or time-series data. RNNs may be recognized by their feedback loops. These learning algorithms generally forecast future events based on time series data. Stock market projections and sales forecasting are examples of use cases, as are ordinal or temporal challenges like language translation, natural language processing (NLP), speech recognition, and picture captioning. These features are frequently integrated into popular apps like Siri, Voice Search, and Google Translate.

RNNs use "memory" by incorporating information from previous inputs to influence the current input and output. Traditional deep neural networks presume that inputs and outputs are independent. However, RNNs' production relies on the sequence's previous components. While future occurrences might also be beneficial in defining the production of a particular sequence, unidirectional recurrent neural networks cannot account for these events in their predictions.

RNNs share parameters across each layer of the network and the same weight parameter inside each layer, which is modified via backpropagation and gradient descent to promote reinforcement learning.

RNNs employ a backpropagation through time (BPTT) technique to calculate gradients, which differs from regular backpropagation in that it is particular to sequence data. BPTT works on the same concepts as classical backpropagation, in which the model trains itself by computing errors between its output and input layers. BPTT varies from the standard technique in that it sums errors at each time step, whereas feedforward networks do not need to total errors because their parameters are not shared between layers.

RNNs have an edge over other neural network types since they handle binary data and store it in memory. RNNs may plan many inputs and outputs; thus, instead of producing only one result for a single input, they can provide one-to-many, many-to-one, or many-to-many outputs.

4.2 AI's Role in Critical Industries

Artificial intelligence (AI) is rapidly becoming a necessary and flawlessly integrated technology for organizations and our daily lives. It can transform the world, from optimizing operations to guiding improved decision-making!

Artificial intelligence has influenced every industry, including banking and finance, healthcare, automobiles, telecommunications, manufacturing, defense and military, entertainment and media, and education. Whether we realize it or not, AI is all around us and plays a significant part in our everyday lives. AI is operating in the background whenever we access our Facebook newsfeed, do a Google query, obtain product information from Amazon, or look for airplane tickets online. It is now well-equipped to help solve crucial business challenges and improve people's lives worldwide.

Artificial Intelligence and Financial Services

Artificial intelligence has a wide range of applications in financial services. The technology is nothing short of a game changer in improving financial service organizations' operating efficiency and lowering fraud rates. As a result, many banks are urged to increase their AI budgets. Chatbots that can answer consumer questions and advise them on personal financial products can dramatically cut banks' overall resource costs because they seldom require human participation. One of the first applications of AI in financial services was ENO, a text-based assistant introduced by Capital One in 2017. Since then, AI has advanced significantly and serves essential consumer and corporate financial applications.

Application of AI in Finance

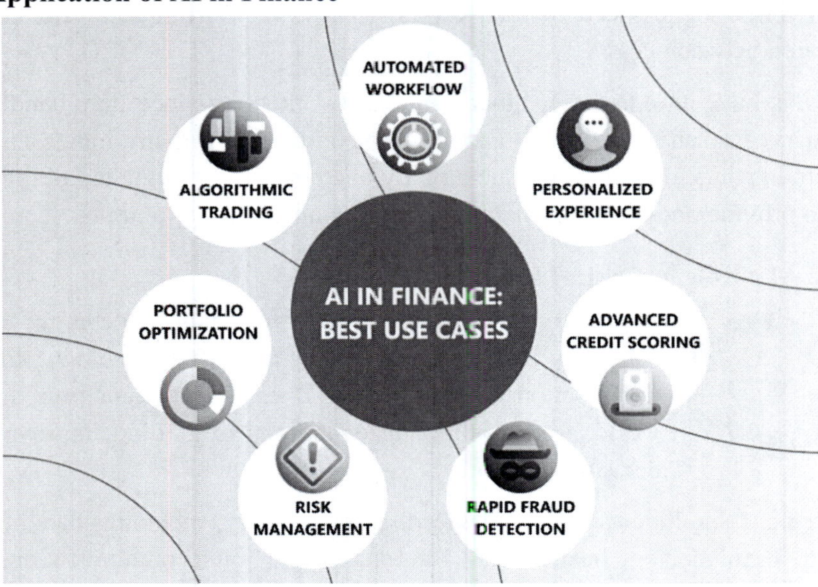

- To assess the risk of insurance

- Fraud detection
- Advanced market insights for investment banking.
- Financial advice.
- Artificial Intelligence and Healthcare

Artificial intelligence has several uses in healthcare. The day when robots perform surgery on humans may not be far off, and what is currently only science fiction may soon become reality. From discovering previously unknown relationships between genetic codes to assisting in the early identification of various disorders, artificial intelligence in healthcare has the potential to alter the industry and how we approach health and medical treatments.

Consider the case of Buoy Health. Patients can enter their symptoms into a chequer chatbot using artificial intelligence technologies. It, in turn, supplies them with the appropriate diagnostic and treatment suggestions. Unsurprisingly, the esteemed Harvard Business School in Boston, Massachusetts, is among Buoy Health's numerous users.

Application of AI in Healthcare

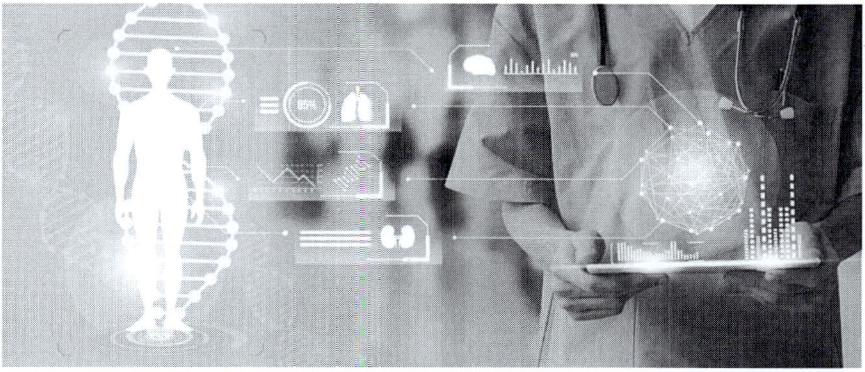

- Insights that confirm the necessity for surgery
- To diagnose infectious illnesses.
- Healthcare applications offer medical aid.
- Wearables driven by AI to track health metrics.
- Possibility of early identification of dementia

- Intelligent robots doing procedures
- To do drug discovery and manufacture.
- Image analysis for medical diagnosis
- Automating superfluous administrative chores.
- Artificial Intelligence for Retail

Consumer behavior and demand essentially shape and drive the retail business. Artificial intelligence technology is causing a significant shift in this area. Artificial intelligence in retail allows retailers to analyze customer demand trends and estimate demand more accurately.

In addition to the aforementioned, technology is being used to assist organizations in optimizing their pricing strategies and product placement. AI in retail may also help retailers manage inventories and reduce overall inventory costs. By utilizing automated merchandise management, merchants can verify that merchandise is placed correctly and that the amount is at different stores and departments.

Application of AI in Retail

- Chatbots can give clever help.
- Algorithms for purchase prognosis
- To derive product prices

- Determining the efficacy of adverts and their optimal placement
- To provide a bespoke in-store experience.
- Artificial Intelligence for Manufacturing

Artificial intelligence technology has enormous promise for increasing automation in the manufacturing business and identifying defects in production processes and units. Over 60% of industrial organizations use AI technology, resulting in less downtime and higher-quality final products. As a result, industrial organizations are implementing AI-based analytics in their information systems to improve worker efficiency. To minimize unexpected machinery damage, manufacturers are employing AI-based predictive maintenance solutions. In the industrial business, AI may assist in maintaining efficiency, detecting faults, and increasing revenues.

Danone Group, a French food manufacturer, uses Machine Learning to improve the effectiveness of their demand forecasts. The adjustment mentioned above had a considerable impact, including a 20% decrease in forecasting mistakes, a 30% decrease in lost revenue, and a 50% reduction in demand planner burden.

Application of AI in Manufacturing

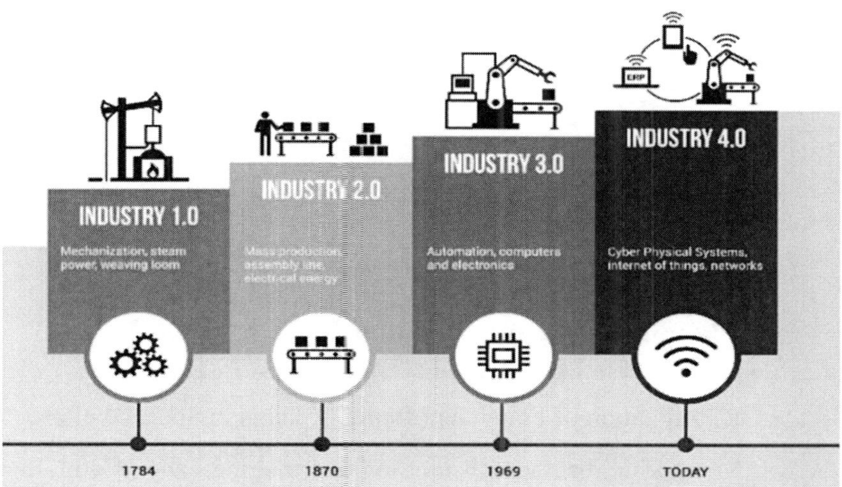

- ➢ Advanced data analytics assists businesses with risk management, data visualization, supply chain management, and the implementation of quick decision-making procedures.
- ➢ Predictive maintenance reduces the chance of system failure.
- ➢ AI and RPA can assist in automating monotonous processes.
- ➢ Inventory management by incorporating AI into current industrial systems.

Artificial Intelligence In Government

The never-ending uses of artificial intelligence technologies are not limited to the business sector. Artificial intelligence in government involves increasing budgetary efficiency, automating regular work, advancing research and development, completing mission-critical duties, and so on. Predicting failure rates has far-reaching consequences, particularly for military equipment and the defense sector. AI also plays a vital role in improving cybersecurity measures for governments constantly under attack from cyber warfare.

Applications of AI by Governments Worldwide

- ➢ Identification of Fraudulent Benefit Claims in Social Welfare
- ➢ Monitoring disease transmission and triaging patients with high-risk scores.

- It is advantageous in home security, where AI may forecast a crime and propose appropriate police presence.
- Use of autonomous military drones in battle
- Self-driving shuttles in preset learned courses such as industrial campuses, city centers, or residential neighborhoods.
- Monitor social media to verify traffic events.
- Classifying emergency calls based on their urgency using voice recognition techniques and machine learning algorithms
- Consider the dryness of woodlands to better forecast wildfires.
- Customer service chatbots and gathering citizen input through social media.
- Document automation, rapid writing of papers and announcements, and document translation

Artificial Intelligence for Education

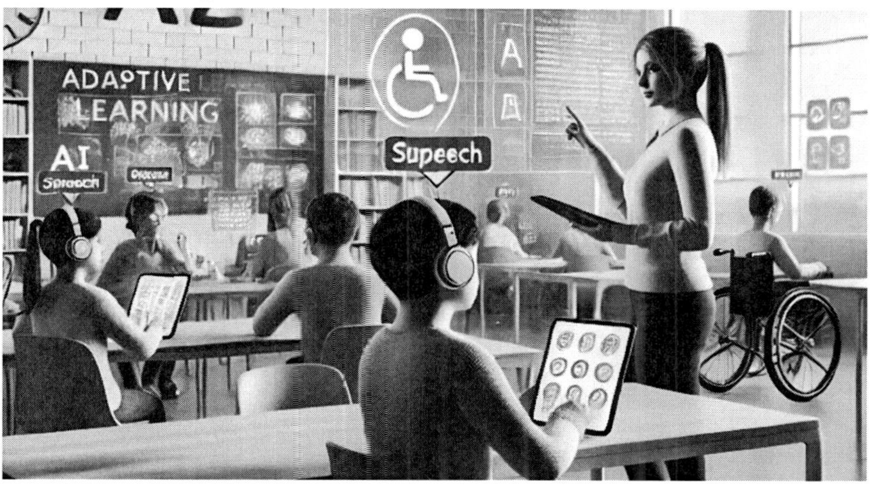

Perhaps one of the most essential uses of artificial intelligence is in education. With the consistent evolution of teaching and learning methods and a rapid shift to virtual modes, particularly amid the ongoing global COVID-19 pandemic, artificial intelligence technology assists educators and students in bridging spatial gaps and using innovative approaches to continue learning.

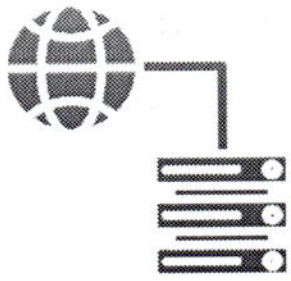

Artificial intelligence in education can help pave the way for more personalized and individualized learning. One of the most important uses of AI in education is extending the fun and power of knowledge to everyone, regardless of where they live or what language they speak. For example, Presentation Translator is a free plug-in for Microsoft PowerPoint that generates subtitles in real time to assist pupils in comprehending what their teacher is saying. The tool above supports around 60 different text languages.

Application of AI in Education

- Personalized education for unique students based on practical learning patterns and current student demands.
- Automate repetitive and monotonous procedures to alleviate the administrative pressure on workers.
- Increasing accessibility through virtual courses that eliminate geographical barriers.
- Self-updating material is more engaging, interactive, and streamlined.
- AI instructors and virtual helpers, like chatbots.

Many more industries are exploring and adopting AI into their systems to improve efficiency, profitability, and quality of life. As we continue to investigate AI, the next blog in the series will focus on AI's most significant application cases today. Stay tuned for more information about AI, and continue to enjoy reading about its various aspects!

4.3 AI Processes and Analyzes Data

AI data analysis is the application of AI tools and data science to enhance the processes of cleaning, examining, and modeling structured and unstructured data. The primary purpose is to unearth helpful information to help develop conclusions and make decisions.

AI helps automate many processes. Organizations may teach a computer program to do the hard lifting instead of having a person look over everything. AI, a simulation of human intelligence, may be used to detect trends and learn from the data on which it is trained to produce correct results.

Understanding the distinction between data analytics and analysis is critical while learning about this topic, even if the two are sometimes used interchangeably. Data analytics is a business intelligence that uses machine learning to derive new insights from data.

Data analysis is analyzing, cleansing, and modeling data to extract usable information, draw conclusions, and make sound decisions. We will walk you through the process.

Data acquisition. Businesses select what they want to learn and then gather data from reliable sources for analysis.

Data cleansing. Data scientists review their data sources to eliminate extraneous information and rectify errors in the raw data.

Data analysis. The analysis procedure occurs once the data has been adequately cleaned. Businesses may utilize this data to identify patterns and derive valuable insights—data interpretation. Trends discovered via data analysis can assist in guiding future business analytics choices.

Common AI Approaches for Data Analysis

There isn't just one technique to approach AI analysis. Depending on your use case, you may include one or more of the AI approaches listed below.

Machine learning. AI uses machine learning algorithms to analyze enormous amounts of data to detect trends and construct AI models. The data provided by the AI model should be relevant to the use case, such as social media posts for sentiment analysis. The machine learning model learns from the information given, presents trends based on what it has learned, and provides appropriate output depending on requests.

Natural Language Processing (NLP).

NLP enables computers to interpret human language. AI systems scan enormous quantities of material to learn word meanings and how to respond to user input. AI may then analyze input text to create new content or summarise old data.

Computer vision is concerned with how computers perceive and interpret pictures and movies. It analyzes massive volumes of picture and video material to identify patterns. AI can detect motion, recognize faces, and extract characteristics from photos.

AI Analytics different from Traditional Analytics

Traditional analytics is frequently a manual process that requires human data analysts to modify data and identify trends. This can be time-consuming, especially when working with significant volumes of data.

AI and machine learning excel at automating much of the data analysis process, allowing them to analyze massive volumes of data faster—and often more correctly than people. AI analytics may discover complicated patterns and deliver predicted insights that manual analysis may not reveal.

Due to processing speed and storage limits, traditional analytics frequently struggles with significant amounts of data. On the other hand, AI analytics can manage and analyze massive volumes of data quickly, making it suited for real-time or near-real-time analysis.

Furthermore, conventional analytics focuses on structured data, such as data organized in rows and columns on a spreadsheet. AI analytics can handle organized and unstructured data (such as text, photos, audio, and video), allowing for a more thorough analysis depending on your measurements and objectives.

Large retail chains are among the companies investing in AI-powered analytics. Walmart, for example, established Walmart Global Tech to assist in personalizing the shopping experience, optimizing packing and shipping, inventory management, and other functions.

Amazon also employs AI analytics for product suggestions, fraud detection, and customer service. Its AI-powered product suggestions are based on various criteria, including consumer purchase history, product reviews, and search history. This enables Amazon to provide consumers with more relevant and personalized suggestions.

Examples of AI Data Analysis

- Now that you've learned what data analysis is and why it's valuable let's examine how businesses utilize AI to enhance analytics.
- Sentiment analysis. Sentiment analysis is gathering information about a topic online and assessing customer responses. AI helps by learning to distinguish between positive, negative, and neutral sentiments and informing businesses on the performance of their brand and products. Netflix is one firm that uses AI for sentiment analysis. It uses AI to detect pain areas and improve the watching experience.
- Predictive analysis and forecasting. AI analytic systems can use historical data, market data, and other variables to estimate future sales and purchase habits. For example, Bank of America uses predictive analytics to better understand the link between equity capital markets (ECM) transactions and investors, allowing the bank to make more targeted presentations.
- Anomaly detection and fraud prevention. Businesses must analyze a large amount of data to detect fraud—but with the increasing number of scams and schemes taking place in the digital age, there is just too much information for people to examine manually. This is where AI can assist. For example, Spotify uses AI to detect fraudulent streaming activities. Their artificial intelligence technology can detect and prevent bot-generated plays by analyzing data such as users' listening patterns and IP addresses.
- Image and video analysis. AI is effective for analyzing photos and videos and informing users about what is occurring with the image. It can locate individuals, check for trends, and even detect illnesses in patient images. Walmart, for example, employs AI to enhance inventory management and loss prevention by analyzing pictures and videos. Walmart's AI systems can recognize goods on shelves, monitor inventory levels, and detect theft.

This chapter covers the basics of AI and machine learning. It explains how deep learning works through neural networks that learn from data. AI's impact on critical industries like healthcare, finance, and manufacturing is highlighted, showing how it optimizes processes and decision-making. The chapter also discusses how AI processes and analyzes data to provide insights, predictive analytics, and real-time decisions.

Part – 2: Major Cybersecurity Risks in AI

Chapter - 5
Data Poisoning Attacks

Chapter 5: Data Poisoning Attacks:

- What is Data Poisoning?
- Direct versus Indirect Data Poisoning Attacks
- Real-World Examples of Data Poisoning

Defence Strategies Against Data Poisoning

5.1 What is Data Poisoning?

Data poisoning, also known as AI poisoning, is a sort of cyberattack that targets training datasets for artificial intelligence (AI) and machine learning (ML) models. The attacker provides false information, alters existing data, or removes critical data points. The attacker's purpose is to mislead the AI into making inaccurate predictions or conclusions.

This manipulation might have far-reaching ramifications across several industries, as the integrity of AI-powered solutions is strongly reliant on the quality of the data on which they are taught.

Why is Data Poisoning a Growing Concern?

As organizations use Generative AI and Large Language Models (LLMs) such as ChatGPT and Google Bard, fraudsters are increasingly taking advantage of the open-source nature of AI datasets. This access allows them to add malicious data into training datasets, resulting in new vulnerabilities.

The incorporation of AI into business not only improves productivity but also encourages cyber criminals to explore novel attack tactics. On the dark web, tools tailored for nefarious usage have evolved, such as FraudGPT and WormGPT. These technologies let fraudsters automate and scale their attacks.

Surprisingly, attackers need to modify a small quantity of data to make an algorithm useless. According to one research, by inserting phrases typically seen in regular emails in spam messages, attackers can fool the system into reclassifying them as safe during the retraining of a fresh dataset.

Data poisoning can develop gradually over time, making it difficult to detect until severe harm has been caused. Attackers may modify progressively information or add noise, frequently without immediate awareness of their activities.

In the healthcare industry, data poisoning can bias diagnostic models, potentially leading to misdiagnosis or incorrect treatment recommendations. For example, if an attacker introduces false data into a model that predicts patient outcomes, it might lead to life-threatening judgments based on inaccurate information.

Similarly, in the financial industry, algorithms that evaluate credit risk or identify fraud are susceptible to data poisoning. Attackers can modify training datasets to construct bogus profiles that avoid detection or accept fraudulent transactions, jeopardizing the integrity of financial systems.

Another business that is highly susceptible to data poisoning is autonomous cars. They rely significantly on precise data for navigation and safety, and data poisoning can cause inaccuracies in sensor data interpretation, resulting in unsafe driving habits or accidents.

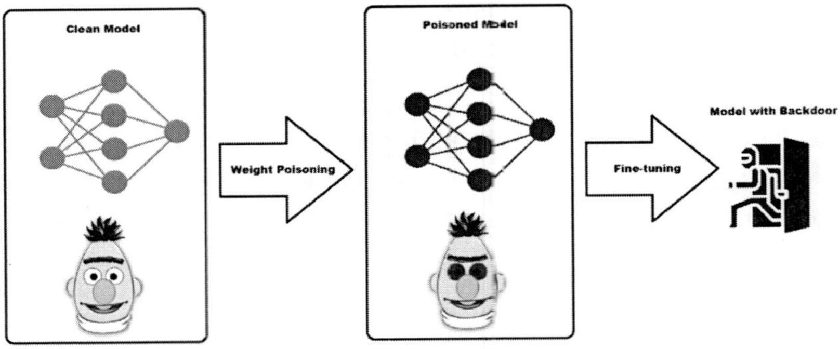

5.2 Direct Versus Indirect Data Poisoning Attacks

Data poisoning attacks are split into two types: direct and indirect assaults.

Direct Data Poisoning Attacks, also known as focused attacks, entail changing the ML model's behavior for specific inputs while maintaining the model's overall performance. The objective is to induce the model to misclassify or misunderstand specific data while maintaining its overall capabilities. For example, consider a face recognition system that is trained to recognize people based on their photos. An attacker might introduce changed pictures of a specific individual into the training dataset, modifying them gradually, such as altering hair color or adding accessories. As a result, when the model comes across a real-world individual, it may misidentify them as someone else due to these targeted alterations.

Indirect Data Poisoning Attacks, also known as non-targeted attacks, try to damage the overall performance of the ML model rather than targeting individual capabilities. This sort of attack involves inserting random noise or irrelevant data into the training set, reducing the model's capacity to generalize from its training data. For example, you may train a spam detection system using a dataset of emails labeled as spam or non-spam. An attacker may inject a large number of irrelevant emails, such as arbitrary text or unrelated content, into the training set. This increase in noise might confuse the model, resulting in a more significant percentage of false positives and negatives. In the end, it will impair its ability to discern between real and spam emails.

The Effects of Data Poisoning on Businesses

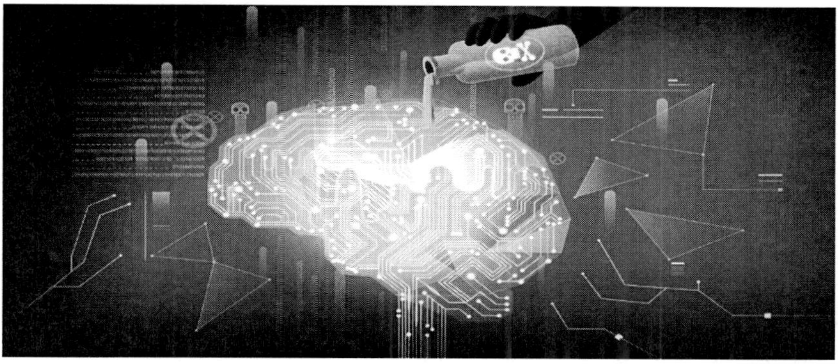

Data poisoning has an impact on modern technology, such as self-driving cars and surgical robots. For example, a National Library of Medicine research found that system mistakes in robotic operations accounted for 7.4% of adverse events, leading to treatment interruptions and more extended recovery periods. These disturbances can raise operating expenses by requiring more extended hospital stays and extra procedures. Furthermore, organizations operating in regulated industries are subject to stringent compliance standards. For example, healthcare organizations must follow the Health Insurance Portability and Accountability Act (HIPAA) and other requirements. A data poisoning incident that results in a data breach or inaccurate medical diagnosis might have serious compliance consequences. The stakes are much more prominent in sectors that use autonomous vehicles (AVs). For example, a data poisoning incident might cause autonomous cars to misread road signs, resulting in accidents and significant liabilities. Tesla drew criticism in 2021 when its AI software misclassified obstructions owing to inaccurate data, resulting in millions of dollars in recalls and regulatory fines.

Data poisoning can cause long-term reputational damage that is difficult to recover from. Incidents stemming from data tampering might damage customer confidence and trust in firms like Tesla, which actively market the safety benefits of their autonomous vehicles. According to a PwC poll, 59% of consumers would avoid using a brand they perceived to be poor in security.

Types of Data Poisoning Attacks

Understanding the various forms of data poisoning attacks is crucial because it allows you to discover weaknesses in artificial intelligence systems. You can put in place robust defenses to prevent malicious actors from manipulating machine learning models.

1. Backdoor Attacks:

A backdoor attack involves embedding hidden triggers inside training data. These triggers are often patterns or characteristics that the model recognizes based on its training but are invisible to the human eye. When the model sees this embedded trigger, it behaves in the way the attacker intended.

These backdoor adversaries enable attackers to circumvent security measures or change outputs undetected until it is too late.

2. Data Injection Attacks:

Data injection happens when harmful samples are introduced into the training dataset with the intention of altering the model's behavior upon deployment. For example, an attacker may introduce biassed data into a financial model, causing it to discriminate against specific demographics during loan processing. For banks, this involves legal issues and a loss of reputation. The problem with these manipulations is that the source of malicious data injection is unknown. The bias becomes obvious gradually, even after the model has been adopted.

3. Mislabelling Attacks:

The attacker manipulates the dataset by giving false labels to a subset of the training data. For example, if a model is being trained to categorize photographs of cats and dogs, the attacker may misidentify images of canines as cats.

The model learns from the damaged data and loses accuracy throughout the deployment, rendering it worthless and unreliable.

4. Data Manipulation Attacks:

Data modification entails modifying the existing data in the training set using various approaches. This involves introducing false data to distort findings, deleting critical data points that would otherwise drive accurate learning, and injecting adversarial samples to cause the model to misclassify or act unexpectedly. If these assaults are not detected during training, they have a significant impact on the ML models' performance.

5.3 Real-World Examples of Data Poisoning

Real-world Examples of Data Poisoning Attacks on Language Models

Data poisoning assaults on language models have been a significant worry in recent years since they potentially jeopardize the accuracy and dependability of these models. In this answer, we'll look at some real-world examples of data poisoning attacks against language models.

Example 1: Poisoning of a Sentiment Analysis Model

One of the first published incidents of data poisoning on a language model occurred in 2019 when researchers showed a data poisoning assault on a sentiment analysis model. The attack entailed introducing a limited number of carefully constructed instances into the training dataset with the intention of leading the model astray and providing inaccurate predictions. The attack's purpose was to cause the model to wrongly identify positive evaluations as unfavorable, which might have significant implications in real-world applications like product recommendation systems.

Example 2: Poisoning the Language Translation Model

In 2020, researchers showed another case of data poisoning on a language model, this time attacking a language translation model. The attack included introducing a small number of samples into the training dataset with the intention of leading the model astray and providing inaccurate translations. The attacker's objective was to cause the model to wrongly translate sensitive information, such as financial or personally identifying information.

Example 3: Poisoning a Text Classification Model

In 2022, researchers revealed another case of data poisoning on a language model, this time on a text classification model. The attack entailed adding a limited number of samples into the training dataset with the intention of confusing the model and causing it to make inaccurate predictions. The attack's purpose was to cause the model to wrongly categorize spam emails as genuine, which might have significant implications in real-world applications like email filtering systems.

Below are some real-world instances of data poisoning threats in federated learning:

Healthcare: In one case, researchers showed a data poisoning assault on a federated learning system intended to predict patient outcomes. The attackers modified the training data by inserting bogus patient records, resulting in a substantial drop in the model's accuracy.

Finance: In another study, researchers demonstrated how a data poisoning assault might be used to corrupt a federated learning system used to assess credit risk. The attackers inserted bogus credit applications, significantly increasing the model's false positive rate.

Transportation: Researchers demonstrated a data poisoning attack on a federated learning system used for traffic prediction. The attackers modified the training data by inserting bogus traffic patterns, resulting in a substantial drop in the model's accuracy.

Effects of Data Poisoning Attacks

Data poisoning attacks in federated learning can have serious repercussions, such as:

Decreased model accuracy: Data poisoning attacks can cause a considerable drop in model accuracy, which can have catastrophic ramifications in a variety of businesses.

Increased false positives: Data poisoning attacks can cause a rise in false positives, resulting in unwarranted interventions or actions.

Loss of Trust: Data poisoning assaults can cause a loss of trust in the federated learning system, with long-term implications for the organization.

Defense Strategies Against Data Poisoning

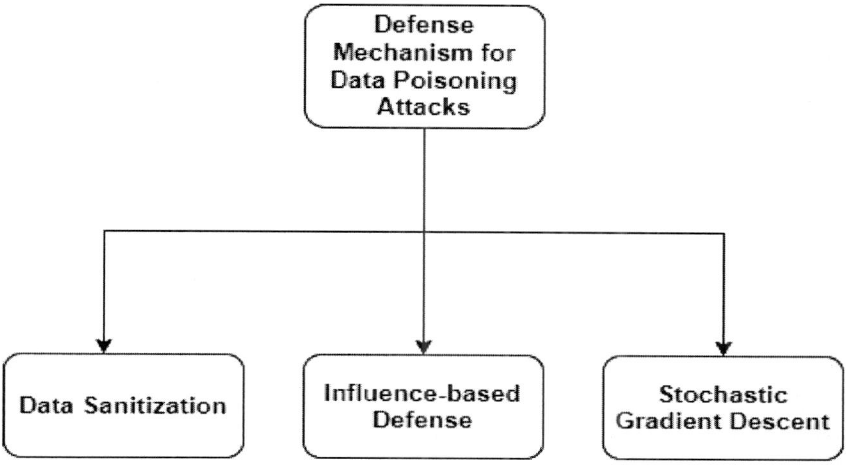

Data poisoning is one of the most pernicious dangers to machine learning (ML) and artificial intelligence (AI) applications. It entails deliberately introducing distorted or misleading data into training datasets, causing models to learn wrong patterns and generate faulty results. Data poisoning may have profound effects, especially in high-risk applications like healthcare, banking, autonomous cars, and cybersecurity. For example, a contaminated dataset in a medical diagnosis system might result in inaccurate treatment recommendations, whilst in finance, it could enable fraudulent transactions. To reduce these risks, firms must implement a multi-layered security plan that includes strong data validation, enhanced detection techniques, and proactive monitoring. This technique guarantees the integrity, dependability, and security of AI systems.

One of the difficulties in protecting against data poisoning is its covert nature. Poisoned data can be challenging to identify, mainly if it is deliberately constructed to appear authentic. Furthermore, the impacts of poisoning may not be evident until the model is deployed, making it difficult to remedy the problem retrospectively. This emphasizes the necessity of proactive defensive techniques that aim to stop poisoning assaults before they cause harm.

Key Defense Strategies

1. Ensure Data Integrity and Quality

The first line of defense against data poisoning is to ensure the integrity and quality of training data. This starts with rigorous data-collecting methods that prioritize reliable sources and enforce strict access rules. Organizations can lessen the probability of harmful actors penetrating the dataset by restricting who can contribute data and carefully screening data sources.

Once the data has been acquired, it must be extensively cleaned and preprocessed to detect and eliminate abnormalities, outliers, and suspicious items. Statistical analysis, grouping, and visualization techniques can be used to discover abnormalities that could suggest poisoning attempts. For example, if a dataset used to train a fraud detection model unexpectedly contains a significant number of transactions with odd features, these entries can be marked for additional inspection.

Data augmentation is another effective method for increasing data quality. Organizations may produce a more diversified and resilient dataset that is less prone to poisoning by creating extra training samples using techniques such as rotation, scaling, or noise addition.

2. Anomaly Detection and Data Sanitisation

Anomaly detection methods are crucial for spotting poisoned data points. These algorithms examine the dataset for patterns that depart considerably from the norm, identifying possible hazards for further examination. For example, if a dataset for training a recommendation system has an abnormally large number of fraudulent reviews, anomaly detection techniques may flag these items as questionable.

Machine learning algorithms may be trained to spot poisoning trends, resulting in a feedback loop that improves detection over time. For example, a model trained to recognize adversarial inputs can be used to filter out poisoned data prior to training.

Data sanitization is another excellent approach for preventing data poisoning. This includes deleting or updating data points that have been detected as harmful or irrelevant. Robust statistics, which are less sensitive to outliers, can be used to mitigate the impact of poisoned data. Furthermore, adversarial training, in which the model is exposed to both clean and poisoned data during training, can strengthen its resistance to poisoning attempts. This method helps the model learn to discriminate between genuine and fraudulent inputs, making it more resistant to future attacks.

3. Federated and Decentralized Training

Federated learning is a new strategy that can considerably lower the danger of data poisoning. Federated learning decentralizes the training process, with models developed on local devices or servers rather than on a centralized dataset. This lowers the likelihood of a single point of failure and makes it more difficult for attackers to poison the entire dataset.

Each local model is trained on its own data, and only model updates (not raw data) are sent to a central server. This means that even if one local dataset is corrupted, the whole model is primarily impacted. Federated learning also improves privacy because raw data never leaves the device, lowering the chance of data breaches.

4. Continuous Monitoring and Auditing

Regular audits and monitoring of the training process are critical for detecting and responding to data poisoning efforts in real-time. Organizations can detect rapid declines in accuracy or strange patterns that signal poisoning by regularly analyzing the dataset and model performance. Automated monitoring technologies can notify administrators of possible dangers, allowing them to take prompt action to limit their impact.

Another excellent practice is to keep track of versioned datasets and model iterations. This allows companies to track out the source of the poisoning and, if required, return to a clean condition. For example, if a model's performance suddenly worsens following the introduction of a new dataset, administrators can discover and delete poisoned data by comparing the new dataset to earlier versions.

Creating a Culture of Security Awareness

Beyond technological measures, building a security-conscious culture inside the firm is critical. Employees who work in data collecting, preprocessing, and model training should be educated to detect the indicators of data poisoning and appreciate the value of data integrity. Straightforward methods for reporting suspicious activities should be developed, and frequent security exercises can assist ensure that teams are adequately prepared to respond to poisoning attempts.

Collaboration with cybersecurity professionals and the larger AI community is also beneficial. Organizations may change their defenses proactively by remaining up to date on the newest poisoning strategies and exchanging information. Open-source tools and frameworks for identifying and mitigating data poisoning are becoming more widely available, allowing businesses to harness their pooled knowledge and skills.

Future Trends in Protecting against Data Poisoning

As the threat landscape changes, new patterns emerge to strengthen defenses against data poisoning. Zero-trust architectures, which remove implicit trust from cloud settings, are gaining popularity as a technique to safeguard AI systems. AI-powered security systems are also under development to detect and respond to attacks in real-time.

Decentralized AI models, developed and deployed on edge devices, improve security by limiting data exposure. Another interesting development is blockchain technology, which creates a transparent and tamper-proof record of data exchanges, allowing for the detection and prevention of poisoning attempts.

Protecting against data poisoning necessitates a comprehensive and proactive approach that includes technological safeguards, ongoing monitoring, and a robust security culture. Organizations may dramatically minimize their vulnerability to poisoning attacks by adopting comprehensive data validation, anomaly detection, data sanitization, and federated learning. Regular audits, engagement with specialists, and staff training all help to reinforce defenses, ensuring that AI systems stay dependable and safe.

As the threat landscape evolves, remaining watchful and adaptable will be critical to ensuring the integrity of machine learning models and the data they rely on. By using these measures, firms may maximize the benefits of AI while reducing the dangers associated with data poisoning.

This chapter explains data poisoning attacks, where malicious data is injected into AI systems to manipulate outcomes. It distinguishes between direct and indirect data poisoning attacks, showing how attackers can either target specific data or subtly influence a system's performance over time. The chapter also provides real-world examples of data poisoning, demonstrating how these attacks have been used in various industries to cause disruptions and degrade system accuracy.

Chapter - 6

Adversarial Attacks on AI Models

Chapter 6

Adversarial Attacks on AI Models

- Understanding Adversarial Machine Learning
- Bias in AI
- Mitigating Adversarial Attacks

6.1 Understanding Adversarial Machine Learning

Adversarial machine learning (AML) is a technique used in machine learning (ML) to deceive or misguide a model using harmful input. While adversarial machine learning has a wide range of applications, it is most typically used to launch an assault or produce a malfunction in a machine learning system. The same technique may be modified to work on many models with different data sets or architectures.

Machine learning models are taught on big datasets related to the subject being studied. For example, if an automaker wanted to introduce an autonomous vehicle how to recognize a stop sign, it would send hundreds of images of stop signs into a machine learning system.

An adversarial ML attack may corrupt the input data, resulting in pictures that are not stop signs but are tagged as such. When the machine learning data-driven application is implemented in practice or production, the algorithm misinterprets the input data, leading the whole system to misidentify stop signs.

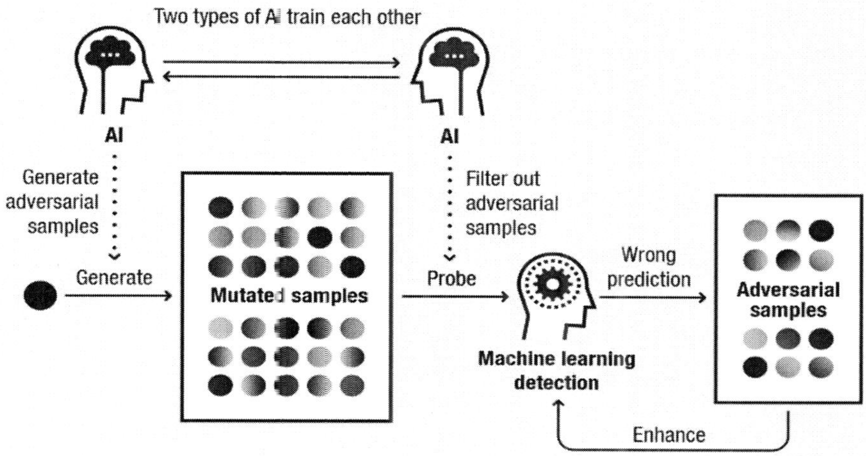

Types of Adversary Machine Learning Attacks

There are three types of adversarial ML attacks. They are carried out in different ways, but the objective is the same: corrupting ML models for malevolent reasons. They include the following:

➢ Evasion Assault

This is the most popular sort of assault variety. Images are modified as input data to fool machine learning algorithms into misclassifying them. This mistake is caused by attackers adding subtle but purposeful noise or perturbations into the incoming data.

➢ Data Poisoning

These attacks occur when an attacker manipulates the ML process by inserting erroneous or poisoned data into a data set, resulting in less accurate results. The purpose of a poisoning assault is to disrupt the machine learning process and reduce the algorithm's utility.

➢ Model Extraction or Theft

An extraction attack occurs when an attacker prods a target model for enough information or data to generate a compelling reconstruction of that model or steals data required to train the model. To avoid this sort of assault, firms must fortify their machine-learning systems.

Attackers can utilize a variety of approaches to target a model. These strategies use the following approaches:

- **Minimising Disturbances**

Attackers utilize as few perturbations as possible when manipulating input data to make their assaults almost undetectable to security

- **Professionals and ML Models**

Attack techniques that adopt this strategy involve restricted memory. Broyden-Fletcher-Goldfarb-Shanno attacks include DeepFool, the Fast Gradient Sign Method, and the Carlini-Wagner assault.

- **Generative Adversarial Networks**

GANs produce adversarial instances to deceive models by having one neural network (the generator) generate bogus examples and then try to trick another neural network (the discriminator) into misclassifying them. While the discriminator improves its classification with time, a GAN improves its ability to generate phony data, which is dangerously effective.

- **Model Querying**

This is the process by which an attacker questions or probes a model to uncover its vulnerabilities and limitations before devising an attack to exploit those flaws. The zeroth-order optimization method is a good illustration of this strategy. It derives its name from the absence of model information and the need to rely on queries.

Defenses Against Hostile Machine Learning

Adversarial ML is viewed by AI and cybersecurity professionals as a developing danger capable of exploiting common flaws in ML systems. Malicious actors have tricked even the most advanced AI systems.

Currently, there is no comprehensive solution to protect against adversarial machine learning attacks. However, there are a few ways that

ML operations teams may employ to assist avoid such an attack. These methods include adversarial training and defensive distillation.

Adversarial Training

Adversarial training is a procedure in which samples of adversarial events are fed into the model and identified as dangerous. This technique helps to prevent hostile assaults, but it requires continual maintenance efforts from data science professionals and engineers who monitor it.

Defensive Distillation

Defensive distillation increases the flexibility of an ML method by allowing one model to anticipate the outputs of a previously trained model. When trained using this method, an algorithm can detect unknown threats.

Defensive distillation is similar to GANs, which combine two neural networks to accelerate ML processes. One model is known as the generator, and it produces fake content that appears to be accurate. The other is known as the discriminator, and it learns to identify and flag phoney content with increasing accuracy over time.

Adversarial White Box Versus Black Box Attacks

Adversarial ML can be categorized as a white or black-box attack. A white box attack allows the attacker to access model parameters and architecture. These are also known as the internal workings of a model that have been maliciously modified or altered to produce incorrect results.

In a black box attack, the attacker does not have access to the model's internal workings and can only view its outputs. While shielding a model's internal workings might prevent attackers from accessing them or make their attempts less successful, it does not render trained models immune to assaults. Even with everything secured but the outputs, attackers may probe a black box model and retrieve enough sensitive data.

Examples of Adversarial Machine Learning:

Specific adversarial examples are likely to confuse ML models rather than humans. While humans can read what a sign says or see what a picture shows, computers can be duped. The hypothetical examples of adversarial attacks include the following:

Images. A picture is sent to an ML model as its input, but attackers tamper with the input data associated with the image, creating noise. As a result, a picture of a lion is misclassified as an elephant. This type of image classification attack is also known as an evasion attack because instead of directly tampering with training data or using another blatant approach, it relies on subtle modifications to inputs that are designed to evade detection.

Emails. Spam and malware emails can appear as benign, masking malicious intent. The spam or malware tricks the ML algorithm into incorrectly classifying incoming emails as safe or not spam.

Signs. A self-driving car uses sensors and ML algorithms to detect and classify objects. However, even minor changes to a stop sign, such as a small sticker, can cause the vehicle's classifier to misinterpret the sign, potentially resulting in an accident.

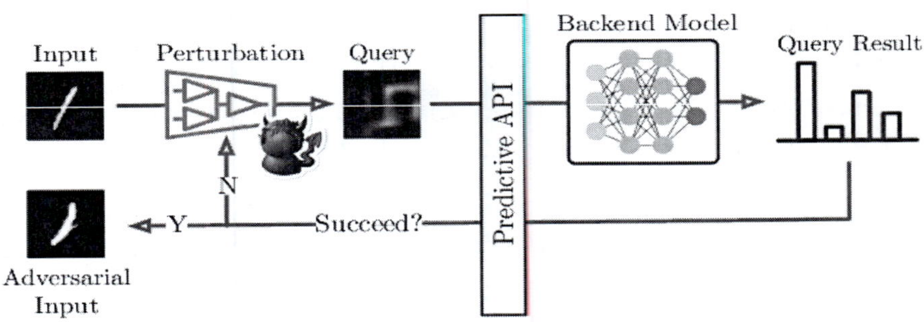

6.2 Bias in AI

The human brain is a complex organ that operates through connections that are both conscious and unconscious. Implicit connections are naturally formed in our brains despite the fact that we may consider explicit prejudice to be unethical. Rather than being something that we can control, this is something that is a natural function of our brains.

When it comes to generative artificial intelligence, it is of the utmost importance to recognize the ways in which these kinds of unconscious connections might influence the model and lead to biased results. We are able to work toward the development of artificial intelligence systems that are more equitable and just if we first identify the origins of prejudice and then provide prompts that are inclusive.

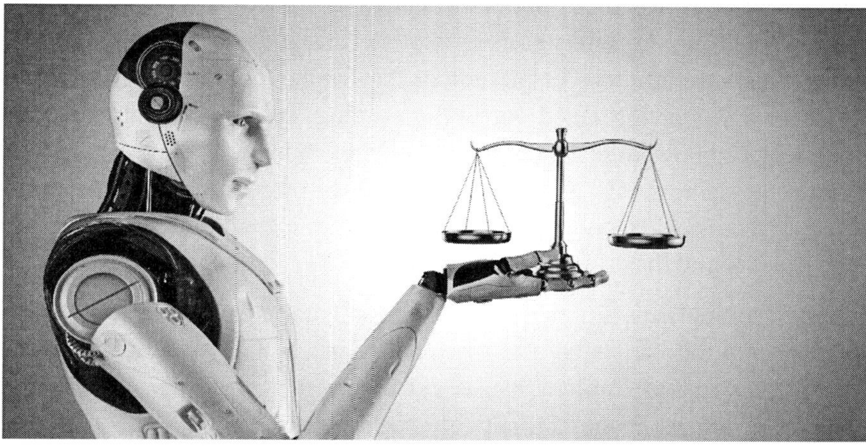

Various Phases in Which Bias May Emerge

It is essential to acknowledge that bias may manifest itself at a number of different stages along the AI pipeline. The gathering of data is one of the key factors that contribute to such bias. If the data that is utilized to train an artificial intelligence system is not varied or representative, then the outputs that are produced may be biased.

When it comes to data collection, bias frequently begins here. If there is a lack of diversity or representation in the data, the artificial intelligence system may provide biased results.

In the event that the annotators have different interpretations of the same label, this might lead to the introduction of bias into the data.

The training phase of the model is essential; if the training data is not balanced or if the architecture of the model is not intended to accommodate various inputs, the model may provide biased outputs.

When the system is deployed, this can potentially result in the introduction of bias if it is not tested with a variety of inputs or monitored for bias after it has been deployed.

As well as Explicit and Implicit Bias:

It is essential to distinguish between apparent biases and implicit ones. The conscious prejudices or views that a person holds with regard to a particular group are referred to as explicit biases. Implicit biases, on the other hand, are attitudes or prejudices that we have without being aware of them and that influence our understanding, behaviors, and decisions without our knowledge. These biases are the outcome of preferences held within the same group and are a reflection of more enormous structural inequalities. We frequently absorb these biases without knowing the prevalent social messages that we come across.

Implicit prejudices are particularly detrimental since they are firmly established and can impact our behavior even when we actively reject them. This makes implicit biases extremely dangerous. We should be careful of our language and actively seek out other opinions in order to lessen the impact of prejudice and to foster a culture that is inclusive and respectful of all different kinds of people.

Varieties of Bias in Artificial Intelligence

When they contribute to social injustice or discrimination, biases can have severe implications that can lead to dire consequences. This is due to the fact that existing prejudices may be strengthened and made worse by skewed data, which ultimately results in systemic inequities. As a result, it is of the utmost importance to maintain vigilance in the process of identifying and correcting biases in data and models, as well as to strive for fairness and impartiality in all decision-making processes that are driven by data.

The phenomenon known as **selection bias** occurs when the data that is used to train an artificial intelligence system is not reflective of the world that it is intended to simulate. It is possible for this to happen for a variety of reasons, including inadequate data, biased sampling, or other variables that may result in a dataset that is not representative of the population. As an illustration, if a model is trained on a dataset that solely contains male employees, for instance, it will not be able to predict the performance of female employees reliably.

The phenomenon known as **confirmation bias** occurs when an artificial intelligence system is programmed to place an excessive amount of weight on pre-existing views or trends in the data. In addition to failing to see new patterns or trends, this might serve to reinforce pre-existing prejudices.

The term "**measurement bias**" refers to the phenomenon that takes place when the data obtained is systematically different from the variables that are of interest. If, for example, a model is trained to predict students' success in an online course, but the data acquired is only from students who have finished the course, then it is possible that the model will not correctly predict the performance of students who drop out of the course.

When an artificial intelligence system perpetuates destructive prejudices, this is an example of **stereotyping bias**. When a language translation system identifies specific languages with certain genders or preconceptions, for instance, or when a facial recognition system gives less accurate results when attempting to identify individuals of race, these are examples of examples of bias.

It is a kind of **out-group homogeneity** bias that occurs when an artificial intelligence system is less capable of discriminating between people who are not a part of the majority group in the training data. This happens when the system is exposed to out-group homogeneity information. When it comes to working with minority populations, this might lead to incorrect classification or inaccurate information.

6.3 Mitigating Adversarial Attacks

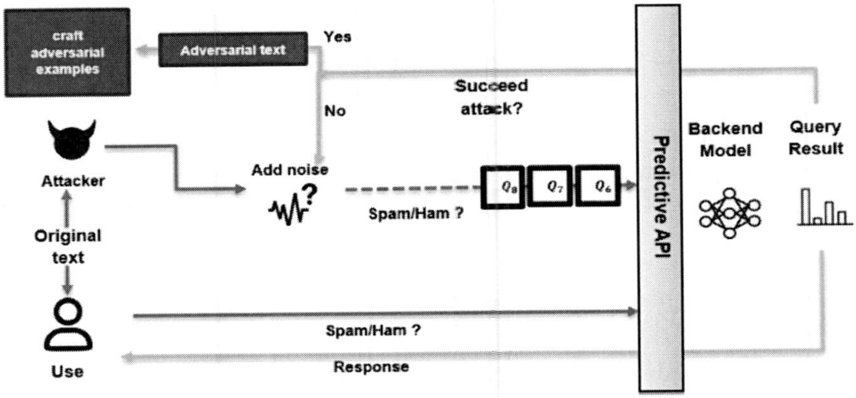

Adversarial AI makes use of the mathematical structure of ML models by addressing inherent flaws in the model's decision limits. Iterative probing is used by attackers to detect small, often unnoticeable changes to input data that lead models astray. By discovering these "blind spots," opponents can precisely reroute model outputs.

Core Mechanism

Identifying vulnerabilities: Attackers examine model responses to a variety of inputs.

Crafting adversarial inputs: Subtle data changes cause model faults.

Adversarial examples are data inputs that are purposely designed to seem normal while causing models to deliver inaccurate results. These perturbations can be as little as modifying a few pixels in a picture or introducing harmless-looking records into a training dataset. Such manipulations jeopardize system integrity by undermining the model's reliability, causing a cascading effect in which strategic errors accumulate quickly and silently. ML models sometimes lack inherent robustness to odd or purposefully prepared data inputs; their learning methods prioritize statistical patterns over deeper semantic comprehension. This limited focus renders them vulnerable to adversarial assaults since they can't tell the difference between a legal input and one designed to deceive.

It is not always simple to tell the difference between inadvertent model flaws and purposeful hostile manipulation. Your whole supply and development chain, from developers to sysadmins to DevOps and cybersecurity/support personnel, should use intense monitoring, anomaly detection, and cross-validation methods. Regular retraining against known adversarial cases, along with human supervision, aids in the differentiation between random model glitches and deliberate attacks. Advanced logging and extensive audit trails might reveal unexpected patterns that are more consistent with malicious intent than with ordinary data anomalies.

Types of Adversarial AI Attacks

Consider an autonomous vehicle's vision system: a white-box attacker with inside knowledge modifies stop sign pictures such that the model interprets them as speed limits, endangering passengers. Meanwhile, a black-box attacker may continually test voice command systems, finally identifying a tiny audio pattern that causes a home assistant to unlock a door. Such occurrences illustrate the practical implications of hostile AI in daily devices.

➢ Evasion Assaults

Evasion attacks avoid detection systems by making subtle changes to inputs. A typical situation is to change malware samples just enough to mislead an antivirus into categorizing them as benign. These assaults are especially effective against models that rely significantly on surface-level characteristics.

➢ Key Risk

Production systems are susceptible because evasion attempts target models that are currently in use.

➢ Effective Defenses

To mitigate manipulation, use adversarial training and rigorous feature extraction.

➢ Poisoning Attacks

The training phase becomes a battleground in poisoning assaults when adversaries feed carefully constructed harmful data into the training set. These inputs disrupt the model's learning process, resulting in reduced accuracy or purposeful weaknesses. Injecting mislabeled spam emails into a dataset, for example, may train a machine to disregard real spam. Training data integrity checks are critical. Combining automatic data validation with human assessment helps prevent fraudulent inputs from reaching the model.

➢ Inference-based Attacks

Some adversarial strategies target the inference stage of ML systems, using outputs to extract sensitive information or learn about the training data. There are two typical approaches:

➢ Model Inversion

Reconstructing sensitive data points (e.g., patient records) from model outputs.

➢ Membership Inference

Identifying if a given data point was included in the training dataset may compromise user privacy.

Both attack types thrive on concrete outputs like likelihood scores. Reducing output granularity and using differential privacy measures dramatically reduces their success rate.

➢ Model Extraction Assaults

In model extraction, attackers repeatedly query a deployed model to simulate its functionality. Over time, they can create a duplicate of the target model, thereby stealing its intellectual property. This assault is particularly problematic for proprietary models used in high-risk applications such as fraud detection or autonomous systems.

Organisations can address this by:

Restricting API Access: Limit your queries to avoid excessive data collection.

Implementing rate limits: Attackers can be slowed down by limiting the amount of queries permitted per user.

Best Methods for Addressing Hostile AI Threats

To mitigate adversarial AI, specialized countermeasures for specific attack types must be combined with more extensive tactics to enhance system resilience:

Defending Against Evasive Assaults

Evasion attacks use surface-level patterns in input data to trick models. Adversarial training improves models by subjecting them to modified inputs while training. Robust feature extraction reduces noise by separating significant patterns in input data while limiting the impact of irrelevant or misleading information, ensuring that predictions are based on accurate signals rather than exploitable artifacts. It is helpful in preventing adversarial assaults, which include introducing minor perturbations or "noise" into inputs to confound the model.

Countering Poisoning Assaults

Poisoning attacks disrupt the training process by introducing harmful data. Automated validation processes and multiple dataset checks assist in assuring data integrity. For example, cross-referencing flagged transactions across several sources helps to keep financial systems clean.

Mitigating Inference-Based Attacks

Inference-based attacks, such as model inversion and membership inference, extract important training information from outputs. Individual data points can be protected while keeping model utility by reducing output granularity and using differential privacy approaches.

Preventing Model Extraction Attacks

Model extraction is the process of repeatedly querying a model to recreate its capabilities. Limiting query speeds and minimizing API output details, such as returning class labels rather than probability, prevent attackers from obtaining the data required for reverse engineering. Logging queries provide additional protection by detecting questionable activities.

Developing a Layered Defensive Plan

Effective defenses frequently involve numerous techniques working together:

Adversarial training involves exposing models to designed instances during training to increase resilience.

Data validation pipelines: Use automated tests to detect and delete fraudulent inputs.

Output obfuscation: Reduce the granularity of model outputs to prevent information leaking.

Rate limiting: Limit the number of queries to discourage model extraction efforts.

Combining these methods with red-teaming exercises and cross-team communication results in a strong, adaptable defense against developing hostile AI threats.

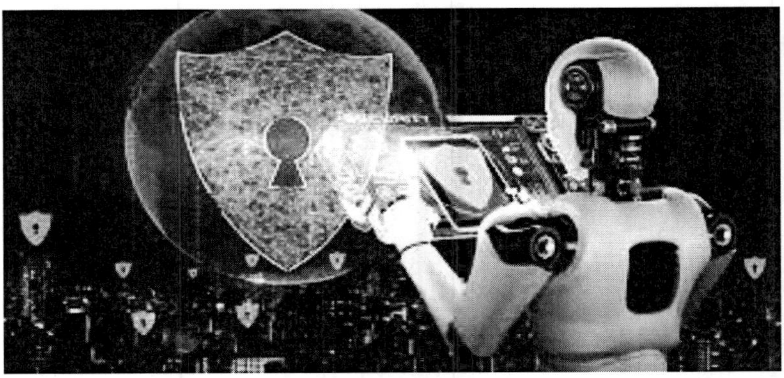

This chapter explores into adversarial machine learning, where attackers manipulate AI models to produce incorrect outcomes. It discusses the issue of bias in AI, highlighting how it can make models more susceptible to adversarial attacks. The chapter concludes by exploring strategies for mitigating these attacks, such as improving model robustness, increasing data diversity, and implementing better training techniques to defend against adversarial manipulation.

Chapter - 7

AI-Powered Social Engineering & Deepfakes

Chapter 7

AI-Powered Social Engineering & Deepfakes

- The Impact of AI on Social Engineering Cyber-Attacks
- The Rise of Deepfake Technology
- Impact of AI-Generated Fake Content
- AI Fraud Detection and Prevention Strategies

7.1The Impact of AI on Social Engineering Cyber-Attacks

Social engineering assaults have long been a danger to enterprises globally, accounting for around 98% of all cyber-attacks. Every year, the average firm experiences around 700 of these attacks. A social engineering assault, whether it takes the form of a clever phishing email or a carefully orchestrated series of contacts between workers and seemingly innocent or "legitimate" individuals with ulterior objectives, can have disastrous repercussions.

The principle of social engineering assaults is similar: criminals try to influence and fool people into disclosing secret or sensitive information or doing activities that might jeopardize an organization's security. It is difficult to detect social engineering assaults since they may be carried out in far more psychologically focused and meticulous methods.

While businesses can invest in advanced cybersecurity and threat detection tools to detect unusual network and system activities, a socially engineered interaction between a hostile actor and an inexperienced employee can go under the radar.

Furthermore, as artificial intelligence (AI) has advanced, social engineering approaches have become more intricate, covert, and more complex to detect. AI's imaginative and quick nature allows attackers to automate, scale up, and fine-tune social engineering attack approaches, unwittingly expanding businesses' attack surfaces. So, how has AI exacerbated the issue of social engineering as a cyber threat, and what can organizations do to address the changing landscape?

The Growing Threat of Social Engineering

Social engineering is simply defined as psychological manipulation strategies used by attackers to mislead victims. It's a game of trust, emotions, and perception, with attributes like curiosity, fear, greed, or a desire to assist being used to lower an individual's guard and, therefore, the organization's.

By appealing to these characteristics, attackers might persuade people to unknowingly grant them access to key systems or extremely sensitive information. Even the most security-conscious and technologically savvy teams might be vulnerable to a clever attack like this. This is why firms have attempted to train their staff and outsourced contractors in critical areas such as DevOps and project management on adequate cyber awareness.

Social engineering is the foundation of several cyber dangers and standard attack methodologies, including (but not limited to):

- Phishing refers to emails, texts, or websites that impersonate reputable sources in order to obtain login credentials or financial information.
- Baiting involves leaving infected physical media, such as USB devices, for victims to find and insert.
- Pretexting is creating settings to lure victims into disclosing sensitive information.

- ➢ Tailgating entails following authorized individuals through protected doors

Digital transformation, increasing connection between geographically dispersed teams, and real-time information sharing have rendered more people vulnerable to social engineering. These assaults have spread to the point that there were 493 million ransomware attacks in 2022 alone, and 19% of all data breaches were caused by stolen or compromised login credentials. All of this boils down to social engineering strategies, which are unlikely to slow down very soon.

Given the increasing frequency and severity of social engineering threats, it's no surprise that many organizations are looking to build better, enterprise-grade cybersecurity solutions and engage in rigorous awareness training. However, it is critical to understand that attackers are beginning to weaponize social engineering with the use of AI, which might pose an even greater set of issues.

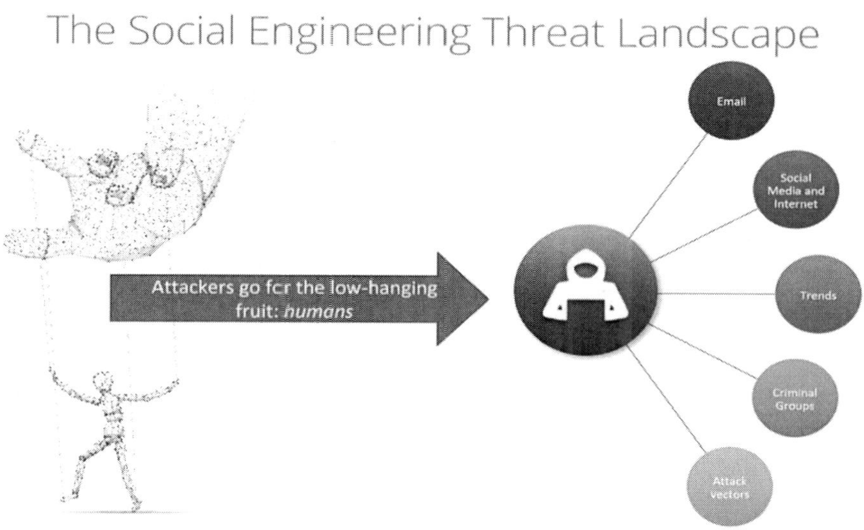

How AI is Increasing Social Engineering Hazards.

The combination of AI's deep-learning algorithms and superior processing capabilities has enabled hostile actors to launch increasingly sophisticated assaults. Such tactics, which were formerly extremely human-led, are becoming increasingly automated, allowing them to avoid many baseline cybersecurity protections.

As AI capabilities advance, attackers use them to augment their attacks in a variety of ways.

Hyper-personalized phishing - Artificial intelligence can scan social media to generate spear phishing emails with recognizable names, logos, and messaging for each target. AI-powered bots infest social media sites, impersonating real users and using convincing language and deepfakes to trick consumers.

Natural language creation - AI can quickly produce meaningful, human-like text and dialogue when urged to sound humanistic. This enables attackers to create compelling social engineering content on a large scale and easily overcome early cautionary measures.

Emotional manipulation: By examining the target's digital trail, AI may determine communication methods, emotional triggers, and weaknesses unique to each victim. This makes deception techniques more effective.

Detection evasion - AI can test and develop social engineering approaches to avoid triggering security alerts and identifying blind spots.

Automated reconnaissance enables AI to swiftly acquire intelligence about targets by scraping data sources such as social media, marketing websites, and public records. This information is used to improve social engineering by spreading disinformation to target specific audiences and blurring the distinction between truth and fake data.

The advent of AI technologies has provided attackers with more excellent weapons for developing targeted, context-aware social engineering strategies on a large scale. They've made it faster, simpler, and cheaper for bad actors to run targeted campaigns. As a result, companies and people have fallen far behind in the race to safeguard defenses effectively.

How does AI-powered Social Engineering Impact Businesses?

With AI intensifying social engineering dangers, firms' attack surfaces are becoming broader. If a company is already vulnerable to a variety of hacks, such as data leaks,

DDoS (distributed denial-of-service), and malware, AI will most certainly cause further problems.

Highly compelling phishing emails, bolstered by convincing AI-generated content, can fool employees into clicking harmful links, downloading files disguised as malware, or entering credentials into fraudulent logins or landing sites. As a result, accounts, networks, and data are increasingly vulnerable to compromise.

AI-generated deepfakes, such as videos, photos, and voice recordings, enable attackers to mimic CEOs and well-known personalities in order to disseminate false information, deceive workers, conduct targeted extortion, or cause disruption.

By analyzing massive databases, AI may improve the content to create enticing discourse for specific audiences, undermining consumer trust and degrading firms' public image. Traditional hacks carry a reputational risk, significantly if customer or stakeholder information is compromised, but AI exacerbates the situation tremendously.

AI's intrinsic capacity to discern patterns might reveal previously unknown system weaknesses. Once entered, AI programs may surreptitiously browse, gather, and export vital data, having successfully avoided early security detection technologies.

These are just a few of the consequences that can impact enterprises. Ongoing awareness and modification to existing protections will be critical in controlling and overcoming these developing hazards.

Mitigating the Hazards of AI Social Engineering.

To increase resilience, companies should update their policies, processes, and technological protections.

Employees who are trained to spot social engineering approaches, particularly those enabled by AI, will be better prepared to face new dangers. Simulated testing and breaches can put their true resilience to the test, allowing them to improve their abilities and awareness.

Accept multi-factor authentication (MFA) as a primary protection strategy. Enforce extra authentication credentials for all users, regardless of seniority. Ensure that any shared logins are confirmed by users who confirm OTPs (one-time passwords) from administrators, biometrics, or security codes. To improve initial account security, consider installing enterprise-grade password management and creation systems that apply minimal requirements and no-reuse restrictions.

Maintain increased email awareness and treat any external interactions with care. Implement DKIM, SPF, and DMARC to authenticate legitimate emails and thoroughly investigate any abnormalities that get through the gaps. Block any dangerous file downloads that come from servers or IP addresses other than those known to the organization.

Perhaps most importantly, enterprises must deploy AI as a security mechanism against technology exploited for nefarious objectives. To keep ahead of illegal AI usage, businesses could consider internal AI uses for predictive and proactive threat neutralization.

Companies that adopt a multi-layered strategy for cyber resilience may more confidently traverse the complicated digital terrain. AI-enabled social engineering risks are expected to increase in frequency and sophistication. Therefore, companies must take proactive actions and be adaptable to assure adequate, strong security.

7.2 The Rise of Deepfake Technology

The digital world is developing dramatically. Deepfake technology is one of the most disruptive developments in recent years. This sophisticated technology has significant ramifications for a variety of industries, notably digital marketing. Understanding how deepfakes affect corporate marketing strategy is critical for both marketers and customers.

The Science behind Deepfakes

Deepfake technology is based on artificial intelligence, specifically the subset known as deep learning. This technology lets computers learn and make judgments using massive volumes of data. Deepfake systems may produce remarkably realistic photos and videos by employing a neural network known as a Generative Adversarial Network (GAN), which convincingly alters faces and sounds.

The learning process incorporates two neural networks: one that creates content and one that analyses it. The generator produces pictures or audio that attempt to replicate actual individuals while the discriminator compares them to legitimate material. This back-and-forth procedure continues until the generator produces enough realistic outputs to fool even experts.

Evolution of Deepfake Technology

As deepfake technology advances, so does the need for legal frameworks that control its usage. The legal environment around deepfakes can be uneven, with rules ranging greatly between regions. Existing copyright, defamation, and privacy regulations in some places may give some protection against dangerous deepfake apps. Deepfake technology evolves, and so does the need for legal frameworks to oversee its usage. The legal environment around deepfakes is still patchwork, with rules ranging widely between nations. Existing copyright, defamation, and privacy regulations in some places may give some protection against dangerous deepfake apps.

Furthermore, the entertainment sector has begun to explore the creative possibilities that deepfake technology offers. Filmmakers can use renowned actors' likenesses to create sequels or spin-offs, allowing beloved tales to continue seamlessly. This has raised debate about the ethical implications of employing such technology, notably around permission and the depiction of persons who may no longer be alive to authorize their digital likenesses. Furthermore, the potential for deepfakes to improve virtual reality experiences is being examined, with the promise of immersing audiences in previously unimaginable ways.

However, the emergence of deepfake technology presents serious issues about disinformation and security. As technology becomes more accessible, the possibility of malevolent usage rises, resulting in misleading information that can influence public opinion or ruin reputations. Governments and organizations are currently wrestling with the difficulty of establishing effective countermeasures to detect and limit the effects of deepfakes while balancing innovation with the requirement for ethical norms in digital media.

Revolutionizing Content Creation

The development of deepfake technologies transformed the content generation process. Marketers can now create customized video commercials showcasing brand ambassadors, celebrities, or even customers—all with the touch of a button. This lowers production costs while allowing firms to adapt to current events and trends.

Consider a hypothetical coffee firm that makes celebration films using a popular local personality promoting its new mix. Using deepfake technology, the company can generate authentic-looking encounters without having the celebrity on-site for filming. This adaptability allows marketers to keep their content current and relevant. Furthermore, the ability to create high-quality video content for a fraction of the previous cost allows even smaller businesses to compete in the digital domain, leveling the playing field and encouraging more incredible innovation throughout the sector.

Personalization Taken to the Next Level

Deepfake technology enables advertisers to produce highly customized content. By studying customer data, marketers may create tailored adverts that address individual tastes and habits. Imagine getting a marketing email with a video in which a brand ambassador addresses you by name, discusses your previous purchases, and recommends new things based on your preferences.

This degree of customization may boost customer engagement and loyalty, giving companies an unprecedented chance to connect meaningfully with their target demographic. Enhanced user experiences resulting from personalized content contribute to excellent conversion rates, making deepfake technology a unique opportunity for digital marketers.

Furthermore, as consumers get more used to personalized experiences, firms that use this technology may foster a feeling of exclusivity and intimacy, strengthening their relationship with customers. As a result, deepfake technology has the ability to completely revolutionize the landscape of digital marketing coving up hitherto inconceivable options for innovation and engagement.

Balancing Innovation with Integrity

While deepfake technology has excellent benefits for digital marketing, it also poses ethical concerns. The ability to produce compelling but wholly fake material might jeopardize the authenticity of messages that companies want to communicate. As customers, we rely on authenticity and transparency, and the abuse of deepfake technology may jeopardize confidence.

Balancing innovation and honesty in marketing is critical. Marketers must use this powerful technology properly to retain customer confidence and loyalty, which may be rapidly eroded by apparent manipulation. The goal is to create a paradigm that values deepfakes' creative potential while prioritizing ethical principles. This might include using prominent disclaimers or labels to warn users when they interact with changed information and establishing a climate of honesty and responsibility.

Potential for Misuse and Deception

Deepfakes are easily weaponized, posing the risk of misuse and deceit. This involves generating fake endorsements or deceptive marketing that may mislead customers. Furthermore, customers may fail to discern between authentic and altered material, driving up the need for openness in digital marketing.

Establishing ethical norms and properly utilizing deepfake technology is critical for protecting brand reputation and consumer confidence. The campaign against disinformation begins with proper marketing techniques.

Furthermore, the consequences of deepfake technology go beyond marketing; they address more significant social concerns, such as the erosion of public faith in media and the possibility of growing cynicism toward all types of digital material. As companies negotiate this complicated terrain, they must consider both the immediate impact of their marketing initiatives and the long-term implications for customer perceptions and societal standards. Engaging in open discussions with consumers about such technology may serve to alleviate worries and develop a more informed audience, eventually leading to a stronger connection between businesses and customers.

Current Regulations and Limitations

The laws governing deepfake technology are still in its infancy. Existing regulations frequently struggle to keep up with the fast evolution of technology. Regulations prioritize consumer protection and advertising requirements, particularly addressing the complexities of deepfake material.

This lack of strong regulation might result in inconsistent standards among industries, generating uncertainty. Without defined policies, companies may unintentionally slip into ethical pitfalls when using deepfake material. For example, a marketing campaign that uses a deepfake of a celebrity may deceive customers about the endorsement, perhaps leading to legal ramifications and harm to the brand's image. The consequences of such activities go beyond the immediate financial impact; they can damage customer trust and lead to a more significant social mistrust of digital media.

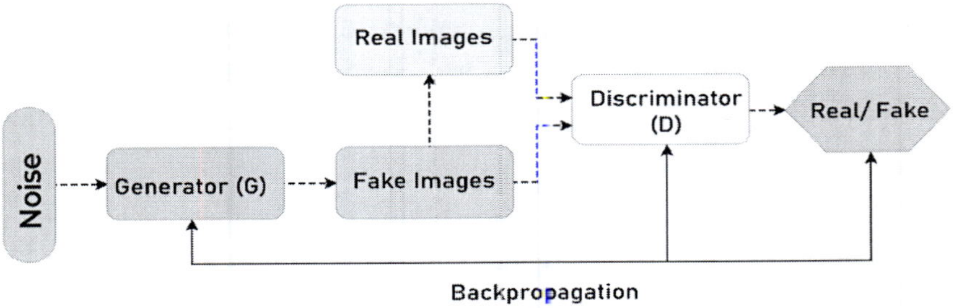

7.3 Impact of AI-Generated Fake Content

Over the past few years, the growth of deepfake material has been exponential, with the number of deepfakes online doubling every six months. According to research, in 2023, roughly 500,000 video and voice deepfakes were shared on social media around the world. By 2025, we can expect to see 8 million deepfakes shared online, consistent with doubling deepfakes every six months.

The ease of access to powerful AI tools and the large quantity of publicly available data contribute to the spread of deepfakes.

Social Media and the Deepfake Explosion

Social media platforms, where the distribution of information is rapid and widespread, play a crucial role in the rise of deepfakes. A study conducted by iProov found that in 2022, less than one-third of global consumers knew what a deepfake was. This highlights the potential for misinformation to spread rapidly through these platforms.

Impacts on Society

The rise of deepfakes poses significant challenges to various parts of society, from politics to business. Here are some key ways in which deepfakes are already impacting our lives:

1. Political Manipulation

Deepfakes have already disrupted political landscapes by showing political figures saying or doing things they never did. One famous example of this involves Ukrainian President Volodymyr Zelenskiy in a deepfake video asking his army to cease fighting. This not only undermines the trust in political leaders but also has the potential to change public opinion and influence elections.

2. Misinformation and Fake News

The rapid spread of deepfakes on social media worsens the already prevalent issue of misinformation. A study conducted by the University of Baltimore and Cybersecurity firm CHEQ found that in 2020, fake news cost the global economy $78 billion.

3. Privacy Concerns

Deepfakes can be used for harmful purposes, such as creating fake content featuring individuals without their consent. A notable example of this is the actors' strike in 2023, where actors protested using AI and deepfakes to use their likeness without their permission. This raises serious privacy concerns and has led to calls for more laws and legislation to protect individuals from deepfake media.

4. Impact on Business

The corporate world is not exempt from the influence of deepfakes. From CEO impersonation for scams to the creation of fraudulent content, businesses face new challenges in protecting their reputation and maintaining trust.

Mitigating the Impact

Addressing the challenges posed by deepfakes requires a central approach involving technological advancements, legislation, and public awareness. Some potential strategies include:

Prevention and Detection Software

Invest in developing and deploying more advanced deepfake detection and prevention technologies to identify and filter out artificial content on various platforms like social media or news sites.

Education and Awareness

Educate the public about the existence of deepfakes and their potential risks. This could involve teaching the public about tools you can use to prevent and detect deepfakes or making sure they use official media channels. Within businesses, employees can take awareness and training courses on the impacts of deepfakes to mitigate damaging personal and professional reputations.

Increased awareness can contribute to a more perceptive audience less prone to manipulation.

Regulation and Legislation

Governments and regulatory bodies should actively work on making, updating, and implementing legislation that addresses the spread of deepfakes, creating clear consequences for those who misuse this technology. One example of this involves the UK Online Safety Bill, which was updated to address better protection of victims of deepfake abuse. To do this globally, collaboration is needed at the international level to address the universal nature of deepfake threats. Sharing information, best practices, and technological advancements among countries can create strong protection against the misuse of deepfakes.

Transparency in Content Creation

Social Media platforms should focus on transparency in content creation, making it easier for users to verify the authenticity of the media they encounter. This may involve watermarking, other certification forms, or using third-party validation tools for media integrity.

The Future of Deepfakes

Deepfakes will continue to evolve and become more sophisticated in the foreseeable future, raising concerns over their societal influence. As AI algorithms advance, the line between authentic and manipulated content blurs, with implications for people, privacy, and trust.

As deepfakes become more convincing, there is a growing risk of losing trust in digital content. People may become skeptical of the authenticity of any video or image, leading to a general atmosphere of doubt. This can have significant implications in high-stakes industries like law enforcement and justice, where evidential integrity is paramount.

The growth of deepfake technology, evident in the surge of shallow fake and deepfake content, highlights the urgency for sophisticated software and legislation. Striking a balance between innovation and safeguarding against harmful misuse will be necessary, requiring a collaborative effort from technology developers, lawmakers, and the public to scrutinize synthetic media. By doing so, we can collectively work towards mitigating the negative impacts of deepfakes and preserving the integrity of our digital world.

Providing Trust and Confidence

Having identified the threat that digital disinformation poses to law enforcement, justice, and investigations, Issured created MeaConnexus. MeaConnexus is a remote video interview platform designed to provide a secure, tamper-evident online interview environment where any party cannot manipulate material without other parties knowing. Therefore, it protects the chain of custody and instills trust and confidence in conducting interviews online.

7.4 AI Fraud Detection and Prevention Strategies

The surge in online transactions has increased the frequency and complexity of fraudulent activity. Cybersecurity defenses are continuously put to the test by innovative strategies designed to circumvent traditional detection methods. Human monitoring, while vital, is no longer adequate to combat the sheer volume of these security breaches; it is challenging to keep up with the speed and ingenuity of current cyber-attacks.

According to research, 37% of participants raised their cybersecurity spending to obtain more powerful security software. AI fraud detection stands out as a significant advancement in the battle against online fraud. Using powerful algorithms, AI systems can swiftly filter through enormous datasets to find abnormal patterns and anomalies that may suggest fraudulent activities. This system improves the detecting process while also learning from each encounter, thereby boosting its prediction skills.

This technology improves security while lowering financial losses, protecting consumer confidence, and ensuring the integrity of corporate processes. This article delves into the mechanics of AI fraud detection, including the benefits and challenges of deploying it, as well as best practices for developing a plan that takes advantage of this technology.

How can artificial intelligence (AI) identify fraud?

AI fraud detection uses machine learning algorithms to examine activities and find abnormalities that may indicate fraud. It begins with creating a baseline of typical transaction patterns and user behaviors. The system then continually analyses the data, looking for departures from the norm. As it meets fresh and diverse data, the AI model refines its parameters, making it more successful at distinguishing between legal and suspect activity.

The processes involved in AI fraud detection include the following:

Data acquisition. Collecting massive volumes of transactional and behavioral data from numerous sources.

Feature engineering. Identifying and choosing data elements or features that may indicate fraudulent conduct.

Model training. Using historical data to train machine learning models to detect fraudulent patterns.

Anomaly detection. Using statistical approaches to detect outliers that deviate from expected trends.

Continuous learning. Updating the model with new data ensures that the system adapts to different fraud strategies.

Alerting and reporting. Detecting suspicious activity and generating comprehensive information for further investigation.

Developing an AI Fraud Detection Technique

When implementing an AI fraud detection strategy, it is critical to take a methodical approach that optimizes the system's efficacy and efficiency. This includes negotiating issues like data quality, integration, and legal compliance, as well as developing a robust operational foundation for the AI system. Consider the following recommended practices:

1. Set up a Cross-functional Fraud Management Team

Putting together a specialized team with personnel from several departments, including IT, data science, compliance, legal, and operations, might be critical. This team should be in charge of overseeing the AI fraud detection system's development and maintenance, ensuring that a variety of views are taken into account and that the system is in line with larger business OKRs.

2. Continuous Monitoring and Updating

AI systems must be regularly checked to ensure they are working as planned. Regular updates and retraining with fresh data are required to provide their efficacy against changing fraud practices. This method should be included in a planned maintenance routine to maintain current and correct AI models.

3. Create a Rigorous Fraud Detection Plan

AI should be part of a multi-layered fraud detection approach. Combine it with additional fraud protection techniques, such as multi-factor authentication, encryption, and anomaly detection systems, to provide a complete defense against fraudulent activity. This comprehensive method ensures that if one layer is hacked, the additional security measures serve as a backup to safeguard against fraud.

4. Invest in the Correct Tools

Invest in the necessary technologies and platforms to meet your AI fraud detection needs. This involves choosing AI frameworks and tools that are well-supported, scalable, and interoperable with your current systems.

5. Engage in Ethical Data Utilization

Ensure that the use of AI in fraud detection adheres to ethical standards and strictly protects customer privacy, not only by implementing transparent data collection practices and ensuring secure storage and handling of sensitive information but also by adhering to stringent data protection laws and regulations.

In the United States, this includes compliance with the Gramm-Leach-Bliley Act (GLBA) for financial information, the Health Insurance Portability and Accountability Act (HIPAA) for health data, and state-level requirements such as the California Consumer Privacy Act (CCPA) for consumer data protection. Furthermore, if the AI system processes data on individuals in the European Union, it must adhere to the GDPR, which sets stringent standards on data consent, rights, and security.

6. Simulate Assaults to Assess Robustness

Regularly recreating fraudulent assaults, such as through penetration testing or red team exercises, is essential for assessing the robustness of AI fraud detection systems. These controlled but realistic attack scenarios can reveal weaknesses in the system's defenses and provide actionable input for strengthening the system against actual fraud attempts. Organizations may remain ahead of the curve by modeling advanced persistent threats and sophisticated fraud strategies.

7. Develop a Culture of Security

Create a security-conscious culture inside your firm by giving particular training that teaches staff how to detect the early symptoms of fraudulent activity, such as phishing attempts or unexpected money demands. Empower each team member with an understanding of their job within the larger context of the company's anti-fraud structure, emphasizing the necessity of adhering to security procedures. This proactive approach to security acts as a human firewall, complementing and improving the technological protections offered by AI detection technologies.

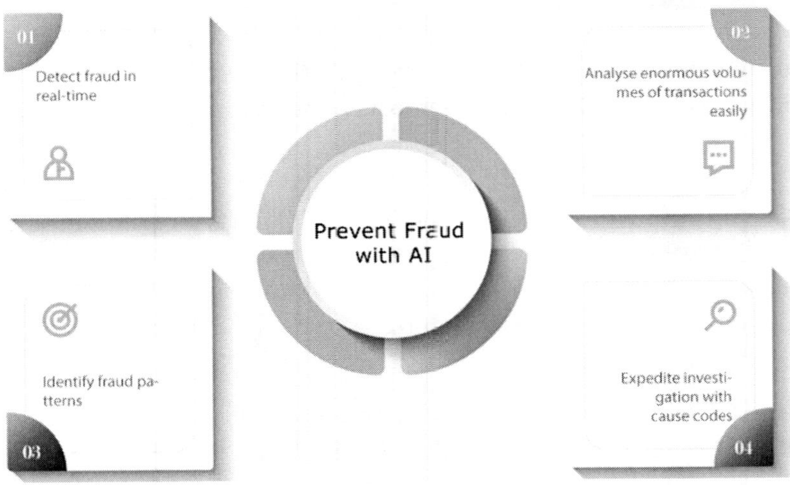

Challenges of AI Fraud Detection

While AI fraud detection technologies provide significant benefits, they also present a number of hurdles that enterprises must overcome. These challenges might vary from technological constraints to regulatory compliance difficulties. Here are some challenges to consider:

Data Quality and Availability

To identify fraud efficiently, AI systems require access to high-quality, relevant data. However, data might be inadequate, out of date, or erroneous, causing AI systems to perform poorly. Furthermore, privacy issues and restrictions may limit the availability of data, making it harder for AI systems to learn from a large dataset. Maintaining data integrity and secure access to critical data while adhering to privacy rules is a difficult balance that must be struck.

Integration with Existing Systems

Integrating AI fraud detection into an organization's existing infrastructure can be a complex process. Legacy systems may not be compatible with the most recent AI business tools and machine learning technologies, necessitating costly updates or even whole overhauls. This integration procedure can be resource-intensive and disruptive, perhaps resulting in downtime or decreased functioning during the transition phase. Businesses must carefully design and execute the integration of AI technologies in order to mitigate these effects.

False Positives and Consumer Friction

AI systems can still produce false positives, identifying legal transactions as fraudulent. This can cause friction for customers, resulting in aggravation and even harming the customer-business relationship. Balancing sensitivity to fraud with the requirement to create a positive customer experience is a constant problem. AI models must be continuously refined in order to eliminate false positives and preserve consumer satisfaction.

Keeping up with Emerging Risks

Fraudsters are continuously devising new methods to evade detection systems. AI models, no matter how powerful, require constant upgrades to stay current with these emerging threats. This necessitates a commitment to continuously training the AI system with the most recent data on fraudulent activity; AI systems cannot be static and must be part of an adaptive and proactive fraud prevention strategy.

Regulatory and Ethical Considerations

Businesses must verify that their AI fraud detection systems comply with all applicable rules, including data protection and privacy legislation such as the General Data Protection Regulation (GDPR). The application of AI in decision-making processes poses ethical concerns, such as the possibility of bias in algorithms, which might result in unjust treatment of specific client segments. Companies must carefully traverse various regulatory and ethical environments in order to remain compliant and ethical.

This chapter examines the impact of AI on social engineering attacks, making them more personalized and effective. It also covers the rise of deepfake technology, highlighting its potential to spread misinformation and manipulate digital content. Finally, the chapter discusses AI-driven fraud detection and prevention strategies, emphasizing the need for both technology and awareness to combat these threats.

Chapter - 8
AI Model Theft and Intellectual Property Risks

Chapter 8

AI Model Theft and Intellectual Property Risks

- Understanding and Preventing AI Model Theft
- Safeguarding Proprietary AI Models

8.1 Understanding and Preventing AI Model Theft

Model theft in artificial intelligence is a developing worry since it may result in significant intellectual property losses and pose a number of security risks. This sort of danger is demonstrated by occurrences such as Tesla's lawsuit against a former engineer. We provide insights into the problems that businesses experience in protecting their AI technology and the strategies they may take to reduce these risks.

The Threat of AI Model Theft

Insiders and competitors find it advantageous to steal AI models and proprietary algorithms. For example, Tesla faced such a threat when a former engineer was sued for allegedly stealing source code from its Autopilot technology before joining Xpeng, a Chinese competitor. This event shows the susceptibility of AI models to theft, as well as the possible consequences for firms' competitiveness and security. For more information on the Tesla event and the larger context of AI model theft, check out articles from Electrek and Yahoo Finance, which give thorough details of the case and its consequences for the industry.

Model theft might result in a loss of competitive edge. The theft of proprietary AI models has a direct influence on a company's market competitiveness. These models frequently reflect major expenditures in R&D, incorporating unique ideas or breakthroughs that distinguish a firm from its competition. Unauthorized purchase and use of these models by rivals can reduce the original company's market share, erode its technological edge, and neutralize its strategic advantages, making it challenging to maintain a distinct value offer in an increasingly competitive field.

The use of stolen AI models for malevolent purposes poses significant security vulnerabilities. Such models can be reverse-engineered to exploit weaknesses in the systems for which they were intended, allowing cyber-attacks such as data breaches, system disruptions, and even espionage. Furthermore, if these models are linked to key infrastructure or used to make personal safety choices, their flaws might have profound effects, including risking lives and jeopardizing national security.

AI model theft may cause financial and reputational damage in addition to the loss of intellectual property. Companies may face costly legal fights to safeguard their assets, potential settlements, and the costs of creating new technologies in order to reclaim their competitive advantage. Furthermore, a breach of trust and a loss of consumer confidence can have long-term consequences for a company's reputation, potentially resulting in lost revenue, reduced brand loyalty, and a decline in shareholder value. The reputational impact may be especially damaging in areas where trust and dependability are critical.

AI model theft has emerged as a serious issue for businesses. The potential to recreate or extract these models via adversarial approaches presents significant risks to intellectual property, competitive advantage, and operational integrity.

In this piece, we'll look at how AI model theft occurs, the repercussions for businesses, and practical ways to protect these critical assets. Check out our piece on How to Secure Large Language Models against Adversarial Attacks and our complete guide on New Risks in the Era of Generative AI for a more in-depth look at the threat environment.

Why AI Model Theft is a Serious Concern.

AI model theft cuts to the heart of an organization's innovation and competitiveness, undermining essential investments in research, development, and deployment. The ramifications of such theft go well beyond financial losses, affecting operational stability, market positioning, and stakeholder confidence.

Key Implications

Intellectual Property Loss: Businesses invest millions in creating and educating LLMs. The theft of these assets enables rivals or bad actors to imitate skills, reducing competitive advantage.

Economic Impact: Replicating an LLM from stolen data removes the major expensive hurdles to model training. This lowers market distinctiveness and might lead to lower profitability.

Reputation and Trust: A stolen or hacked model may result in unlawful use of the enterprise's name, harming consumer trust and brand reputation.

Security Breach: The theft of proprietary LLMs can lead to additional cybersecurity threats, including data modification, disinformation production, or hostile outputs disguised as company systems.

Strategies for Preventing AI Model Theft

Preventing AI model theft necessitates a multilayered security strategy that includes technological solutions, strong governance, and proactive monitoring. Here are six actionable strategies:

Implement API Access Controls

Implement strong authentication techniques like API keys, OAuth, or JWT to ensure only authorized users interact with your models. Enhance this protection with rate limiting to minimize query overload, reduce the possibility of model extraction, and maintain speed.

Integrate Model Watermarking

Incorporate invisible digital watermarks into your AI outputs to track and identify illicit use while preserving model functioning. Choose modern watermarking techniques that resist manipulation and may be used as legal proof if theft occurs.

Use Differential Privacy

Incorporate controlled noise into model outputs to conceal critical parameters, guaranteeing that attackers cannot deduce private data from repeated queries. Optimize this method to balance privacy protection and the accuracy and dependability required for valid use cases.

Deploy AI Gateways

Centralize your security approach by implementing an AI gateway that screens, monitors, and safeguards all interactions with your models. Enhance protection with integrated features such as real-time anomaly detection, fast moderation, and adaptive access restrictions to provide a comprehensive defense against various threats.

Adopt Adversarial Testing

Perform simulated model extraction attacks in controlled situations to proactively detect system weaknesses. Continuously update your testing processes to address the most recent attack vectors, ensuring your LLMs stay strong and safe over time.

Promote Organizational Awareness

Educate staff on the dangers of AI model theft, highlighting the importance of intellectual property and everyone's role in its protection. Create complete regulations that govern access and behavior, limiting internal and external risks to your AI assets.

Emerging Trends in AI Model Theft Prevention

Adversaries' strategies change in lockstep with the AI landscape. Staying ahead of these dangers necessitates strong security measures and a proactive strategy. Here are some new developments in AI model theft protection that businesses should constantly monitor:

Federated Learning for Decentralized Training

Training models on different devices without sharing raw data reduces exposure to sensitive parameters.

Blockchain for Enhanced Model Security: Creates an immutable record of ownership and access, making every interaction traceable and secure.

Advanced Threat Intelligence Integration: Uses continually updated intelligence systems to fight developing hostile tactics.

Zero-Trust Architecture for AI Systems: Reduces reliance on implicit trust by verifying every interaction, lowering internal and external threats risks.

AI-powered intrusion detection uses models trained on adversarial patterns to detect and respond to suspicious activity in real-time.

AI models' growing value and complexity necessitate stronger security measures to safeguard these digital assets. Incidents like Tesla's demonstrate the importance of vigilance and a multifaceted strategy to protect AI systems against theft and unlawful usage. As AI advances, preserving these technical wonders and ensuring their potential is used for good is critical.

8.2 Safeguarding Proprietary AI Models

A few significant firms, including Google, Meta, and Hugging Face, are responsible for training and publicly distributing massive pre-trained models, which serve as the foundation for various applications. However, embracing these open-source solutions entails significant privacy and security concerns that are frequently neglected. This paper provides a complete review of the typical privacy and security risks associated with employing open-source models.

The area of artificial intelligence (AI) has made significant progress in recent years thanks to the broad use of open-source machine learning models in both academia and industry. Given the resource-intensive nature of training on large datasets, many applications use pre-trained models provided by a few significant companies. However, embracing these open-source solutions entails substantial privacy and security concerns that are frequently neglected. Successful privacy and security assaults have many consequences, from minor inconveniences like service disruptions to extremely concerning situations such as bodily injury or the disclosure of sensitive user data.

This paper provides a complete review of the leading privacy and security risks associated with open-source models. They are increasing awareness about these risks to encourage safe and secure usage of AI technologies.

Understanding Security and Privacy Risks for Open Source Models

Open-source models are frequently released on sites like Hugging Face, TensorFlow Hub, and PyTorch Hub, and they are used in various applications and environments. While this method has apparent benefits, the reliability of such pre-trained open-source models is becoming increasingly important. Because the model architecture, weights, and training technique are public knowledge, hostile adversaries have an advantage when attempting to attack these models instead of circumstances where models are maintained behind closed doors. Whereas all of the attacks outlined in this paper are conceivable to some extent without complete model access and knowledge of the unique architecture, they are fundamentally more difficult to execute without such information.

Open-Source Models Leak Private Information

Model Inversion Attacks

Model inversion and reconstruction attacks seek to extract sensitive information from an already trained model's training data, such as by reconstructing pictures that reveal sensitive properties or producing text using private information included in the training data. These attacks rely on generative models to create samples from the training data domain. Model inversion attacks threaten data privacy training since attackers can access open-source models. Consider an open-source model trained to recognize face traits such as hair and eye color. An adversary that successfully executes a model inversion attack may subsequently build synthetic face photographs that betray the identity of individuals from the training data. Data leakage caused by accidental memorizing is closely connected to model inversion attacks. For example, the model may mistakenly finish the query "My social security number" with a valid number found in the model's training data. In addition to unintentional memory leaks, there is fear that malevolent users may purposefully create queries encouraging this type of leakage.

Membership Inference Attacks

Inversion and data leakage attacks attempt to infer information about training data by recreating portions. In contrast, membership inference attacks attempt to determine which data samples were used to train a model. Assume that a hospital is training a machine learning model using medical data from hospital patients to predict if future patients will get cancer. An attacker gains access to the model and obtains private data samples. The adversary attempts to determine if a person's data was utilized to train the cancer prediction model. If the attack is effective, the attacker is aware that the individual not only has or has cancer but was also a patient at that hospital. Full access to an open-source model makes membership inference assaults more possible than models protected by APIs. This is because the attacker can see the intermediate activations of each input, making it more straightforward to determine membership.

Open-source Models are More Susceptible to Security Attacks

Backdoor Attacks

Open-source models are trained on massive datasets containing millions or even billions of data samples. Due to the large scale, human data review is not practicable, mandating dependence on the databases' integrity. However, past research has shown that adding a tiny collection of altered data to a model's training data can considerably impact its behavior. This dataset manipulation is known as data poisoning. Modifying less than 10% of the available data is sufficient for many applications /to teach the model some new hidden features. Such hidden features are known as backdoors, and they are triggered when the model input during inference has a specific trigger pattern. For example, in image classification, trigger patterns might be specific color patterns put in the corners of an image, such as a checkerboard pattern. One famous example is text-to-image synthesis models, which require minor changes to the training data to provide backdoors that may be triggered by single letters or phrases. As a result, these triggered models may produce dangerous or objectionable information. Users find detecting this model tampering complex since the models typically work when given a clean input.

Adversarial Examples

Adversarial attacks target models just during inference instead of poisoning attacks, which alter the training process to inject secret backdoor functions into a model. Adversarial examples are modest modifications to model inputs designed to change the model's behavior for the given input. As a result, these samples can be used to avoid a model's detection and lead to sample misclassification. The fact that open-source model weights and architectures are publicly available creates a risk since adversaries can exploit the model locally and then use manufactured adversarial instances to fool the target model.

Public access to model weights can significantly enable privacy attacks such as inversion or membership inference, mainly if the training set stays private. Similarly, security attacks designed to undermine model resilience can be carried out by altering training data to add secret backdoor functions or creating adversarial instances to affect inference outputs. These hazards affect the published model and the applications and systems that use it. The benefits of releasing huge models, such as large language and text-to-image synthesis models, far exceed the disadvantages. Still, consumers and publishers must be mindful of the inherent hazards associated with open-source approaches. The authors expect that by raising awareness of these vulnerabilities, defenses, and countermeasures may be enhanced, allowing for the safe and private use of open-source models.

This chapter focuses on the risks of AI model theft, explaining how proprietary AI models can be stolen or misused. It explores methods for preventing such theft and safeguarding intellectual property. Key strategies include securing model access, implementing encryption, and monitoring for unauthorized usage to protect valuable AI assets.

Chapter - 9

Privacy and Ethical Risks of AI

Chapter 9

Privacy and Ethical Risks of AI

- Understanding AI Privacy
- Major Issues with AI and Privacy
- How Data Collection Causes AI Privacy Issues
- Real-World Examples of AI and Privacy Concerns

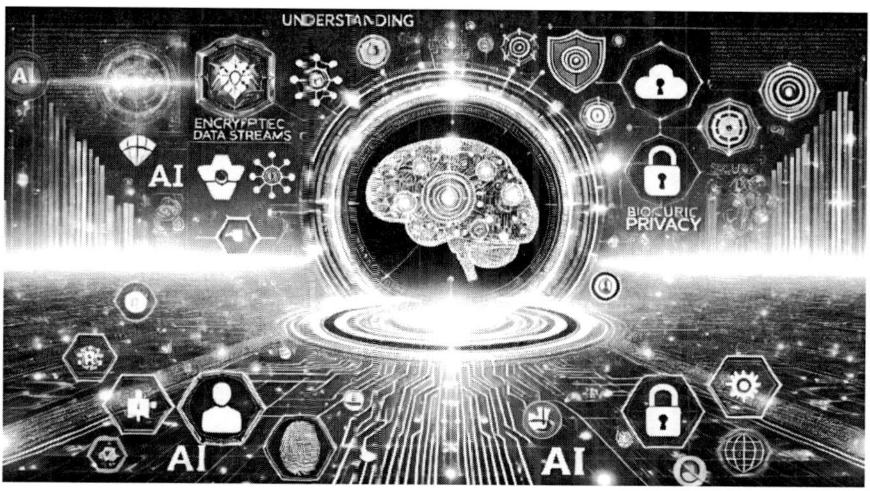

9.1 Understanding AI Privacy

The collecting and utilization of personal data for AI has increased dramatically. AI systems capture vast amounts of data from social media interactions and innovative gadgets to improve user experiences, customize content, and drive targeted advertising. Such extensive data collection raises significant privacy problems. Understanding how AI gathers and handles your data might help you traverse the digital world more safely and make more informed decisions about your online activities.

AI systems collect data on your activities on social media platforms and websites, such as likes, shares, comments, page views, and link clicks. These interactions assist AI in understanding your preferences and interests, allowing it to tailor content and advertising efforts.

AI uses facial and speech recognition algorithms to evaluate pictures, videos, and audio recordings. This data enables AI to recognize (to some extent) the apparent emotions of the people in the videos and the places where they were shot.

Machine Learning Algorithms: These algorithms analyze enormous amounts of data to anticipate actions and tailor experiences. By analyzing previous data, AI can forecast your future actions or preferences and tailor online content, adverts, and other recommendations to your requirements.

Surveillance and smart devices capture sensor data, including location and activity information. GPS and other location-tracking technologies monitor user movements, while smart home devices that automate chores record daily habits and routines.

Websites employ cookies and tracking technology to track user browsing history and provide relevant advertisements. Cookies track website visits, allowing AI to understand online behavior better and provide customized adverts based on the user's browsing history.

9.2 Major Issues with AI and Privacy

Given the fast growth of artificial intelligence, it's not unexpected that difficulties such as improper data integration, ambiguous data regulations, and weak regulatory controls have produced substantial AI and privacy risks.

Unauthorized Incorporation of User Data

When AI model users provide their data in queries, such data may become part of the model's future training dataset. When this occurs, the data might appear as outputs for other users' searches, which is especially dangerous if users have entered sensitive information into the system.

Unregulated Use of Biometric Data

Instead of more traditional means of identity verification, many personal gadgets employ face recognition, fingerprints, voice recognition, and other biometric data security measures. Public surveillance systems are also starting to utilize AI to check for biometric data and instantly identify persons. Many people are unaware that their biometric data is actively gathered, retained, and used for further purposes.

Covert Metadata Collection Practices

When a user interacts with an ad, a TikTok or other social media video, or almost any significant online site, the information from that interaction, as well as the user's search history and interests, may be saved for future more accurate content targeting. While most user sites have policies that address data-collecting procedures and/or require users to opt in, they are only discussed briefly. In the context of other policy texts, most users are unaware of the standards to which they have consented.

AI models have limited built-in security features.

While some AI providers may opt to integrate baseline cybersecurity features and protections into their models, many AI models lack native cybersecurity measures. Even AI technology with rudimentary precautions seldom provides full cybersecurity measures. This is because developing a better and more secure model may be time-consuming and expensive for AI engineers.

Extended and Unclear Data Storage Policies

Many AI companies are unclear about how long, where, and why they maintain user data, whether they keep it for a prolonged period or utilize it in ways that do not value privacy. OpenAI's privacy policy, for example, allows diverse vendors, including cloud and online analytics companies, to access and handle user data as needed. It also includes unnamed parties in the wide "among others" category, which raises data privacy concerns. While OpenAI allows users to view, delete, or restrict data processing, privacy controls are limited, particularly for Free and plan users, making some data usage practices unknown.

Lack of Regard for Copyright and Intellectual Property Laws

AI models typically use training data acquired from the internet, which may contain copyrighted information, and some AI businesses either ignore or disregard copyright and intellectual property laws in the process. AI picture-generating platforms such as Stability AI, Midjourney, DeviantArt, and Runway AI have faced legal action for extracting copyrighted photos from the internet without the permission of their original artists. Some providers argue that existing restrictions do not specifically ban this kind of AI training. As AI models advance, restricting the use of copyrighted information may become more widespread, making it more difficult for developers to identify the origins and licensing of the data their models utilize.

Limited Regulatory Safeguards

Some nations and regulatory agencies are developing AI rules and safe usage policies. Still, there are no overarching formal standards to hold AI suppliers accountable for how they create and use artificial intelligence systems. The most privacy-focused policy is the EU AI Act, which goes into effect on August 1, 2024. Some provisions of the law will take up to three years to enforce. With such lax oversight, several AI suppliers have faced criticism for intellectual property infringement and opaque training and data-collecting practices, but little has come of these charges. In most situations, AI suppliers create data storage, cybersecurity, and user policies without intervention.

9.3 How Data Collection Causes AI Privacy Issues

Unfortunately, the sheer volume and variety of data collection methods almost guarantee that it will be used irresponsibly. Our life revolves around data-collecting initiatives, from web scraping to biometric technologies to IoT devices.

Web scraping harvests content from publicly available internet sources, including third-party websites, wikis, and digital libraries. User metadata is also increasingly being extracted from marketing and advertising databases and websites, including information on targeted audiences and what they interact with the most.

User Queries in AI Models Retain Data: When a user enters a query or other data into an AI model, most AI models save that information for at least a few days. While the data may never be utilized for anything else, many artificial intelligence applications collect and retain it for later training.

Biometric technology may be intrusive: Surveillance equipment such as security cameras, facial and fingerprint scanners, and microphones can all be used to capture biometric data and identify people without their knowledge or consent. Companies can gather, keep, and utilize this information without obtaining customers' permission.

IoT Sensors and Devices are Always On: Internet of Things (IoT) sensors and edge computing devices collect vast volumes of real-time data and analyze it locally to fulfill larger and faster computational tasks. AI software frequently uses an IoT system's rich database, collecting pertinent data via data learning, data intake, secure IoT protocols and gateways, and APIs.

PIs link with various applications, allowing users to effortlessly collect and combine data for AI research and training. Users may gather data from CRMs, databases, data warehouses, and cloud-based and on-premises systems using the appropriate API and configuration.

Public Records Are Easily Accessible: Whether digital or not, public records are frequently gathered and included in AI training sets. Information on public companies, current and historical events, criminal records, immigration paperwork, and other public information can be obtained without prior authorization.

User Surveys Drive Personalization: Although surveys and questionnaires are an old data-collecting strategy, AI providers continue using them to acquire consumer data. Users may answer questions about what material they're most interested in, what they need help with, or anything else that will help the AI better personalize encounters.

Emerging trends in AI and privacy

Because the AI ecosystem is continuously growing, so are the new trends defining AI and privacy problems. Significant developments in AI technology, the increase of legislation, and the influence of public opinion in AI's evolution are among the most important trends.

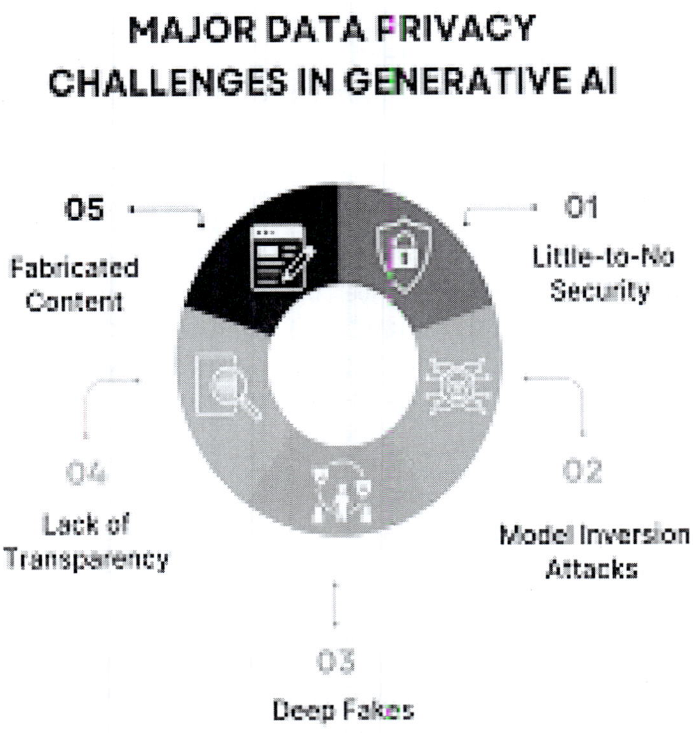

Advancements in AI Technology

AI software has grown dramatically in terms of technological sophistication, application cases, and public interest and awareness. This increase has occurred in classical AI, machine learning technologies, and generative AI. Generative AI's large language models (LLMs) and other huge-scale AI technologies are trained on vast datasets that include internet data and more private or proprietary data. While data collecting and training procedures have advanced, AI companies and their models are frequently opaque about their training or the mathematical processes they employ to get responses.

To address this issue, several generative AI businesses have modified their privacy rules and data collecting and storage requirements. Others, such as Anthropic and Google, have attempted to generate and publish thorough studies demonstrating how they incorporate more explainable AI practices into their AI models, improving transparency and ethical data usage.

9.4 Real-World Examples of AI and Privacy Concerns

While numerous major and widely known security breaches employing AI technology have happened, several vendors and businesses are making substantial progress toward improved data protection. The instances below include both failures and accomplishments.

High-Profile Privacy Concerns with AI

The following are some of the most serious breaches and privacy infractions that have directly included AI technology in recent years:

Microsoft: Microsoft's recent announcement of the Recall feature, which allows business leaders to collect, save, and review screenshots of user activity on their devices, drew criticism for its lack of privacy design elements, as well as the company's recent security breaches. Microsoft will now make it easier for users to opt in or out of the process, and it promises to increase data security with just-in-time decryption and encrypted search index databases.

OpenAI's first significant outage occurred in March 2023, caused by a flaw that exposed certain users' conversation history, financial information, and other sensitive data to unauthorized users.

Google: A former Google employee took AI trade secrets and data and shared it with the People's Republic of China. While this does not necessarily impact personal data privacy, it is disturbing that workers of technology companies have such access to extremely sensitive information.

Successful AI Implementations with Strong Privacy Protections.

Many AI startups are working to provide privacy-by-design AI systems that benefit both enterprises and consumers. These include:

Anthropic: Anthropic has continued to work on its constitutional AI strategy, improving model safety and transparency. The firm also has a responsible scaling strategy, which requires it to frequently test and communicate with the public how well its models perform against biological, cyber, and other essential security parameters.

MOSTLY AI: AI is one of numerous AI providers that have created complete synthetic data-generating technology that safeguards original data from excessive use and disclosure. The technology benefits ethical AI and ML development, data sharing, testing, and quality assurance.

Glean: One of the most popular AI corporate search solutions on the market, Glean was built with security and privacy at its heart. It supports zero trust security, user authentication, the concept of least privilege, GDPR compliance, and data encryption at rest and in transit.

Hippocratic AI is a generative AI program created specifically for healthcare services. It conforms with HIPAA and has been thoroughly vetted by nurses, physicians, health systems, and payor partners to guarantee that privacy is respected and patient data is handled ethically during patient care.

Simplified is an AI-powered insurance claim and document processing system that uses a privacy-by-design strategy to secure its client's sensitive financial information. Its privacy procedures include data masking, restricted storage periods, frequent data erasure, a built-in platform, network and data security components, and data encryption.

Best Practices for Addressing AI and Privacy Issues

While AI offers a variety of tough privacy challenges, firms may address these concerns by implementing the following data governance best practices, adopting proper data usage rules, and educating all stakeholders:

Invest in Data Governance and Security Tools: Extended detection and response (XDR), data loss prevention, and threat intelligence and monitoring software are all effective options for securing AI tools and the rest of your attack surface.

Establish an Appropriate Use Policy for AI: Managers and employees should know what data they may use and how to utilize it when working with AI tools.

Read the Fine Print: All users should review the AI governance documentation carefully for any red flags. They should contact a representative for clarification if they are unsure about something or find it confusing in their policy documents.

Use Only Non-Sensitive Data: For every AI use case that involves sensitive data, firms must devise a secure means to finish the task utilizing digital twins, data anonymization, or synthetic data.

Educate Stakeholders and Users on Privacy: Depending on their degree of access, your organization's stakeholders and workers should be given general and specialized training on data protection and privacy.

Enhance Built-In Security Features: To increase your model's security features, prioritize data security by boosting methods such as data masking, data anonymization, and synthetic data utilization; moreover, consider investing in complete AI cybersecurity tool sets for protection.

Proactively Implement Stricter Regulatory Measures: Establish and enforce clear data usage policies, allow users to submit comments and concerns, and analyze how AI and training data may be utilized without jeopardizing industry-specific standards or customer expectations.

Improve Data Utilization Transparency: Being open about data utilization offers clients more trust in your solutions while providing the information required for AI vendors to pass a data and compliance assessment.

Reduce Data Storage Periods: Limiting data storage periods to the required time for training and quality assurance will help secure data from unwanted access. It also provides users more peace of mind knowing that this restricted data storage policy is in place.

Ensure Compliance with Copyright and IP Laws: While current regulations governing how AI can incorporate copyrighted content and other intellectual property are hazy, AI vendors will improve their reputation (and be better prepared for future regulations) if they regulate and monitor their content sources from the start.

Artificial intelligence (AI) has altered decision-making in various fields, including healthcare, banking, criminal justice, and education. AI-powered decision-making systems offer speed, precision, and scalability but create serious ethical issues. As these systems have more influence on crucial parts of human existence, it is necessary to address the ethical implications to assure justice, transparency, accountability, and respect for human rights. This conversation delves into the major ethical concerns of AI-driven decision-making and suggests solutions.

Bias and Fairness in AI Systems

Bias is a major ethical challenge in AI-driven decision-making. AI systems learn from data; if the training data has biases, the system will most likely maintain or even increase them. For example, face recognition technologies have been demonstrated to have greater mistake rates for individuals of race, resulting in unequal treatment in law enforcement and security applications. Similarly, AI systems employed in recruiting procedures may favor particular demographics over others if the training data reflects prior hiring prejudices.

Addressing prejudice demands a multifaceted approach. First, companies must guarantee that their training datasets are varied and reflective of the communities that the AI system will serve. This includes aggressively detecting and reducing biases in the data-gathering process. Second, developers should use fairness-aware algorithms to account for and mitigate bias during model training. Finally, frequent audits and testing of AI systems may aid in identifying and correcting any biases that may arise over time.

Transparency and Explain ability

Another ethical concern is the lack of openness and explain ability in AI-powered decision-making. Many AI systems, especially those based on deep learning, function as "black boxes," meaning humans cannot simply grasp their decision-making processes. This lack of transparency may be problematic in high-stakes applications like medical diagnosis and criminal sentencing, where people have the right to know how choices that impact their lives are made.

To overcome this, businesses should emphasize the development of explainable artificial intelligence (XAI) technologies. These systems are intended to offer clear and understandable explanations for their conclusions, allowing users to comprehend and trust the results. For example, a loan approval system should be able to explain why an application was denied, mentioning particular characteristics like credit history or income level. Transparency also entails explaining AI systems' limits and possible threats to users, ensuring they are fully aware of how the technology operates.

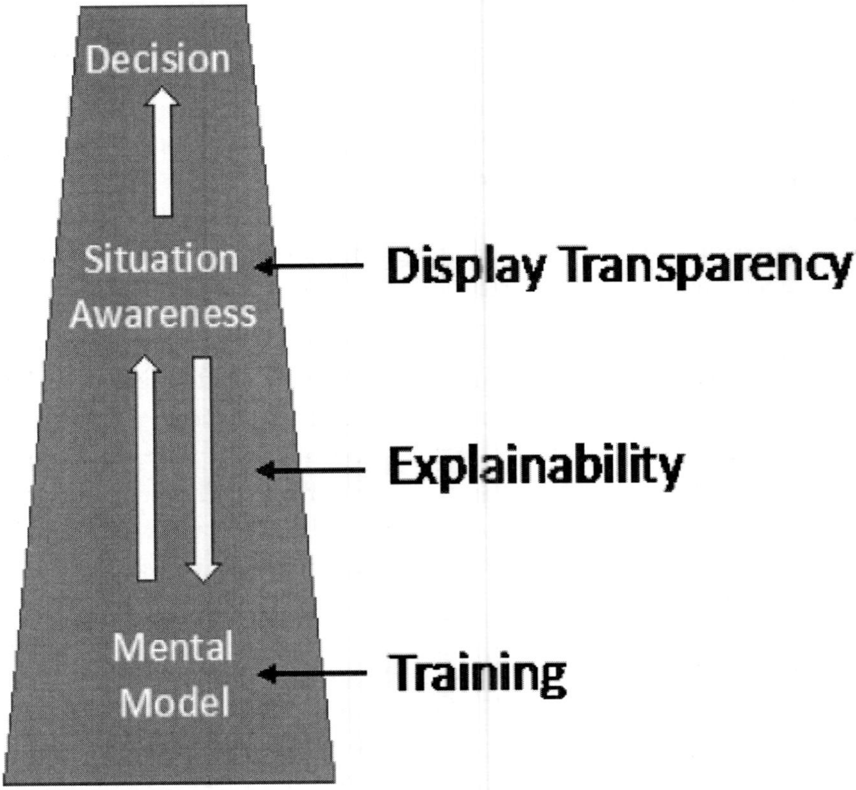

Accountability & Responsibility

AI-driven decision-making presents complex issues of accountability and responsibility. When an AI system makes a mistake or causes injury, it might be challenging to define who is to blame: the developer, the company that deployed the system, or the AI itself. This problem is fundamental in autonomous systems like self-driving vehicles, where AI judgments might have fatal effects.

To guarantee accountability, clear standards and regulations must be developed that specify the duties and obligations of all parties engaged in developing and deploying AI systems. Developers should be held responsible for ensuring their systems are secure, dependable, and without harmful biases. Organizations that install AI systems must accept responsibility for monitoring their performance and resolving any possible difficulties. Furthermore, legal structures should be modified to accommodate the particular issues brought by AI, ensuring that victims of AI-related damage have access to remedies.

Privacy and Data Protection

AI systems depend on massive volumes of data to perform properly, creating serious worries about privacy and data security. The collection, storage, and use of personal data by AI systems may result in infringement of privacy rights, especially if the data is used without the individual's permission or for reasons other than those intended. For example, AI-powered surveillance systems may violate people's privacy rights by collecting and analyzing data without their permission.

To safeguard privacy, corporations must follow stringent data protection requirements, such as the General Data Protection Regulation (GDPR) in the European Union. These rules compel businesses to seek people's express agreement before collecting personal data and to use the data exclusively for certain reasons. Organizations should also employ strong data security procedures to avoid unwanted access and breaches. Data anonymization and differential privacy techniques may also safeguard people's identities while doing extracting important insights from the data.

Autonomy and Human Oversight

AI-powered decision-making systems have the potential to undermine human autonomy by making choices on behalf of people without their knowledge or agreement. This is especially worrisome in fields like healthcare, where AI systems may prescribe treatments or diagnoses without discussing or considering the patient's choices. Similarly, AI systems employed in criminal justice might affect sentence choices without proper human monitoring, resulting in results that are seen as unfair or unjust.

AI systems should be intended to supplement, rather than replace, human decision-making to maintain human autonomy. This entails keeping people in the loop and being able to evaluate, dispute, and overturn AI-generated choices. For example, a doctor should be able to utilize an AI system's suggestions to help them make a diagnosis, but they should still have the ultimate word on the proper therapy. Human supervision is especially critical in high-stakes applications, where AI blunders might have serious implications.

Social Impact and Inequality

The broad use of AI-powered decision-making systems can potentially worsen social disparities. For example, if AI systems utilized in employment, financing, and housing choices are not built and executed with equality in mind, underrepresented groups may suffer disproportionately. Furthermore, the advantages of AI technology are often concentrated in the hands of a few major firms, increasing the disparity between those who have access to AI-driven solutions and those who do not.

To address these issues, politicians and organizations must collaborate to guarantee that AI technologies are created and used in ways that promote social fairness. This involves investing in AI education and training programs to ensure everyone has the necessary skills to participate in the AI-driven economy. It also entails enacting laws that promote fair distribution of AI advantages, such as AI adoption subsidies in underprivileged areas.

Ethics Frameworks and Governance

To negotiate the complex ethical issues of AI-powered decision-making, enterprises should implement ethical frameworks and governance structures emphasizing human values and rights. These frameworks should be created via inclusive and participatory procedures that include feedback from stakeholders, including ethicists, technologists, politicians, and representatives from impacted communities.

Ethical frameworks should explain concepts like justice, openness, responsibility, and privacy while explicitly directing AI system development and implementation. Governance frameworks, such as ethics boards and monitoring committees, may assist in guaranteeing that these principles are followed in reality. These organizations should be able to examine and approve AI initiatives, oversee their execution, and resolve any emerging ethical issues.

AI-driven decision-making has enormous promise for increasing efficiency, accuracy, and scalability in various applications. However, it creates substantial ethical concerns that must be addressed to guarantee that the technology is utilized responsibly and moderately. Organizations may reap the advantages of AI while mitigating its hazards by focusing on justice, transparency, responsibility, privacy, and human supervision.

Finally, the ethical use of AI-driven decision-making requires a collaborative effort by developers, organizations, politicians, and society. By collaborating to develop ethical frameworks and governance structures, we can guarantee that AI technologies serve the greater good while upholding the values that characterize our humanity.

This chapter addresses the privacy concerns surrounding AI, focusing on how AI systems collect and use personal data. It highlights major issues such as data breaches, surveillance, and consent. The chapter also explores real-world examples where AI has raised privacy concerns, emphasizing the need for ethical practices and better data protection.

Chapter - 10

Supply Chain Security for AI Systems

Chapter 10:

Supply Chain Security for AI Systems

- Understanding AI Supply Chain Risks
- Third-Party Dependencies and Security Weaknesses
- Strategies for Securing AI Supply Chains

10.1 Understanding AI Supply Chain Risks

Supply chain management is crucial for guaranteeing a smooth flow of goods and services from manufacturers to end users. Using AI in supply chain management has created new opportunities for organizations to optimize their operations. However, it brings several novel fraud risks that must be handled to maintain the integrity of supply chain systems.

High initial investment and implementation costs

Adopting AI in Supply Chain Management (SCM) might be pricey. Initial investments include AI technologies and implementation-related expenses such as infrastructure changes and people training.

Larger firms may find these expenses bearable, but smaller businesses may face severe financial difficulties. However, it is crucial to note that while the initial expenses may be significant, the potential for long-term operating efficiency and cost savings may offset this. In this instance, rigorous budgetary planning and ROI analysis are critical.

Technology and Personnel Readiness

Incorporating AI into SCM requires a strong technology foundation and a well-prepared HR team. This includes the necessity for staff who are proficient in AI technology or can be trained.

In addition, the organization's technology architecture must be strong enough to handle AI applications without sacrificing performance. Staff will require continuing training and development to stay up with AI progress, adding another layer of investment and complexity.

Data Management Challenges

AI thrives on data, but managing that data isn't always easy. The division of data in many businesses might make it difficult to gather data for AI applications.

Cross-departmental collaboration is frequently required, which can strain resources and impede progress. Efficient and safe data management is critical, particularly given the sensitive nature of supply chain data. Implementing AI might result in disconnected insights and security problems without a strong data management strategy.

Dependency on Vendor Services and Customisation

Another danger associated with AI deployment in supply chain management is vendor lock-in. While vendor services might provide effective AI solutions, businesses may unduly rely on a single vendor's technology and services.

The prospect of restricted flexibility may also reduce the application's efficacy, preventing firms from fully tailoring the technology to their specific needs. As a result, cautious and educated vendor selection based on flexibility and customization choices is critical to effective AI adoption.

Uncertainty and unpredictability of AI technologies

Despite numerous breakthroughs in AI, it retains an element of unpredictability. AI algorithms develop and adapt over time, and their conclusions may occasionally differ from human expectations.

Inaccuracies in AI predictions and choices are unavoidable and can seriously affect the supply chain. This unpredictability emphasizes the significance of human oversight and management in AI-integrated SCM, which may assess, guide, and, if required, correct AI-driven judgments.

Fraud Risks in AI-Powered Supply Chain Management

- **Data manipulation**

AI uses large datasets to develop insights and make informed judgments. Fraudsters may falsify data inputs to AI systems, resulting in erroneous projections, demand forecasts, and inventory management, which disrupts the supply chain.

- **Cybersecurity Threats**

As AI systems process sensitive and secret data, they are great targets for hackers. A successful hack may jeopardize supply chain data integrity, allowing unauthorized access to pricing information, customer data, and trade secrets.

- **Algorithmic manipulation**

Fraudsters can use AI systems by carefully changing parameters to influence supply chain results in their favor. This might result in biased decision-making, such as inefficient supplier selections or favoring specific vendors.

- **Supply Chain Visibility**

AI can improve supply chain visibility, but that same visibility can also reveal risks. Fraudsters may use this transparency to gain insight into supply chain processes and discover weaknesses for future assaults.

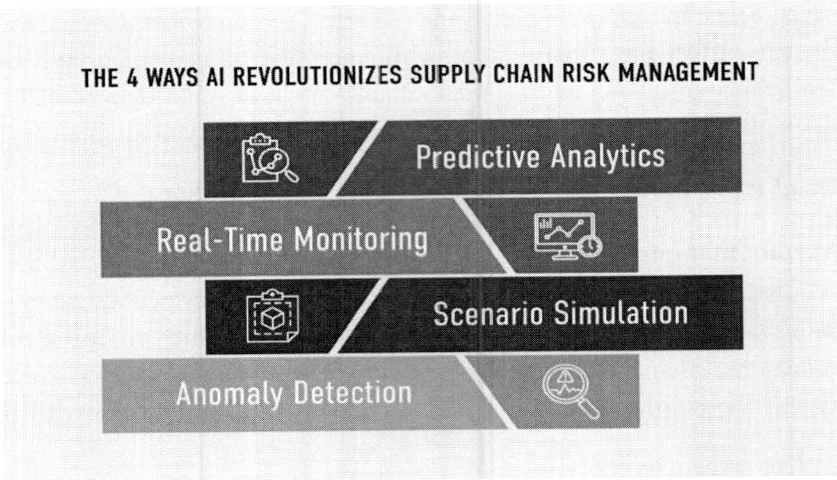

10.2 Third-Party Dependencies and Security Weaknesses

The software supply chain serves as the foundation for current company operations. It is a complicated network of third-party components, libraries, scripts, and processes that power software systems together. While these components improve functionality and efficiency, they also create a complex web of dependencies that can be difficult to manage. Every third-party component introduces a unique set of vulnerabilities and dangers that, if not managed effectively, might jeopardize the entire system.

The diversity of the components' sources adds to the complexity of software supply chains. Developers frequently use open-source libraries and third-party vendors to speed up innovation, but this method might unintentionally introduce unverified and potentially malicious code into their systems. Understanding the complex interplay of these components is critical for organizations seeking to safeguard their software environments while maintaining operational integrity.

Identifying Risks in Third-party Software Dependencies

Using third-party software components exposes an organization's IT infrastructure to various dangers that can jeopardize its security and functionality. One of the most serious dangers comes from vulnerabilities in these third-party components. Unpatched software can be an easy target for attackers, who use these flaws to access systems and steal valuable data. Furthermore, the lack of transparency into the origins of software code raises worries about the reliability of these components.

Another danger is a lack of transparency in software companies' security policies. Organizations frequently have a limited understanding of how these vendors manage and safeguard their code during distribution. This lack of transparency can lead to attackers intercepting and modifying software, inserting malicious code that can remain undiscovered for extended periods. Organizations must conduct comprehensive audits of their third-party dependencies to mitigate these risks, ensuring that only trusted and certified components are included in their systems.

Why is Asset Visibility Important for Security?

Asset visibility is a critical component of operating a secure software environment. Organizations that do not have a clear picture of what is running on their servers are open to possible threats that could jeopardize their operations. Asset visibility entails having a complete picture of all files, scripts, libraries, processes, and executables in an organization's IT infrastructure. This insight enables organizations to discover unauthorized or suspect components representing a system risk.

Full asset visibility allows organizations to establish a baseline of typical operations, making detecting anomalies and potential risks easier. This proactive approach allows IT teams to respond quickly to security issues, reducing their impact on business operations. Additionally, asset visibility aids compliance by verifying that all software components fulfill regulatory requirements and follow best security practices.

Improving System Integrity to Protect Servers.

System integrity is a vital component of any effective cybersecurity approach. It entails ensuring that all software components in an organization's IT infrastructure are reliable and not tampered with. Improving system integrity necessitates combining technologies and techniques that check the legitimacy and reputation of executables, processes, and scripts executing on servers.

Organizations can improve system integrity by using automated verification procedures that determine the origin of all software components. These measures assist in identifying any unauthorized changes or alterations to the software, allowing IT staff to handle possible issues before they cause harm. Furthermore, vulnerability prevention methods can protect systems from known threats, improving the organization's security posture.

Mitigating risks in third-party software supply chains necessitates a multifaceted approach integrating technology, processes, and collaboration. Organizations should start by conducting extensive assessments of their software components, identifying and prioritizing the vulnerabilities that must be fixed. Implementing strong asset visibility solutions is critical for maintaining a clear perspective of the organization's IT infrastructure and recognizing potential dangers.

Case Studies of AI Supply Chain Attacks

- **Case Study #1: SolarWinds Attack**

The December 2020 infiltration is a well-known example of a supply chain attack, which may have involved AI technologies. The attackers targeted Orion software, which is used by many organizations, including national governments in the US and UK, and the world's top 500 companies (Oliver & Patel, 2023). The intricate intrusion allowed fraudsters to compromise unauthorized networks worldwide, resulting in significant data loss and vulnerabilities. Although AI was not used in this case, it can help with future attacks by identifying vulnerabilities in software update mechanisms and determining the optimal time to insert code (Oliver & Patel, 2023). SolarWinds' occurrences demonstrate the vulnerability of software distribution methods. Real-time monitoring of updates can effectively prevent such incidents.

- **Case Study #2: Kaseya Ransomware Attack**

The 2021 Kaseya ransomware outbreak highlighted the negative impact of cyber-attacks on third-party vendors. Breach actors exploited vulnerabilities in Kaseya's VSA software, which MSPs utilize to remotely control clients' IT equipment. By using the VSA platform, attackers were able to send ransomware to hundreds of organizations, harming hundreds of businesses worldwide (Wang & Lee, 2022).

This assault exposed flaws in supply chain ecosystems where a central program supports numerous organizations. In the future, advances in artificial intelligence-enabled intrusions may allow cyber criminals to use machine learning routines to hack across software vendors and coordinate large-scale ransomware attacks during periods of lax monitoring (Wang & Lee, 2022). Kaseya demonstrates the vulnerability of supply chain technologies to attacks, emphasizing the importance of enforcing security measures for third-party applications.

- **Case Study #3: NotPetya Attack**

The 2017 NotPetya assault demonstrated the potential for a single entry point to disrupt the whole supply chain without artificial intelligence. The attack began with MeDoc, a Ukrainian tax preparation software, and spread globally to disrupt organizations in numerous industries, including shipping, medicines, and logistics. Malware masquerading as legitimate software has caused widespread damage, affecting billions of businesses. AI could have improved attackers' target selection and adaptive positioning strategies, thereby increasing the scale and impact of the attack (Jiang & Wu, 2022). The NotPetya attack highlights the need for real-time safeguards to protect clients and suppliers using trustworthy third-party apps.

- **Case Study 4: A Target Data Breach via HVAC Vendor.**

Target's 2013 data breach involving a third-party HVAC provider is a well-known supply chain attack. Attackers could use this vendor to access Target's POS systems and steal credit card information from millions of customers (Smith et al., 2022). The Target attack predates current AI approaches, yet enhanced automation can detect and prevent similar breaches in the future. According to Smith et al. (2022), criminal actors may have scheduled their Vendor system breaches at the optimal period for testing and exploitation. The instance highlights the importance of implementing strong security measures for all vendors, regardless of their strategic relevance for revenue development.

10.3 Strategies for Securing AI Supply Chains

Artificial intelligence (AI) has enormous potential to transform supply chain operations by improving demand forecasting, optimizing inventory management, and streamlining logistics, resulting in more resilient and agile operations. To obtain a competitive advantage, many organizations use AI before verifying the security of their supply chain systems.

AI-enabled systems can expose substantial vulnerabilities, such as data breaches, biased decision-making, and increased costs, without adequate data safeguards. These flaws can disrupt vital operations, ruin reputations, and undermine customer trust, creating long-term damage to the company.

Organizations should approach AI with a security-first perspective to ensure data integrity and customer trust. These three strategies can help.

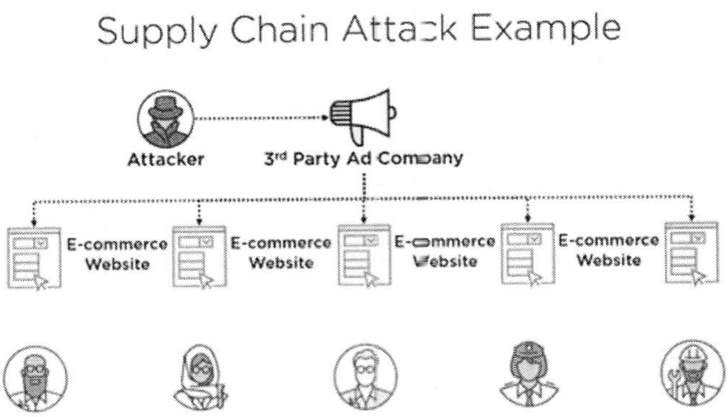

1. Perform a risk assessment to understand data security.

A risk assessment will determine which systems and intellectual property are most valuable to your firm. Furthermore, the risk assessment will determine what data is vital to your organization and where it is stored. Once identified, cybersecurity threats can be prioritized according to their likelihood of occurrence and impact on your business. Then, you may use your prioritized risk list to develop effective reaction plans.

Understanding how cyber-attacks can affect your firm will allow you to offer time-sensitive actions for usage in a multi-layered defense plan. Consider breaking into Fort Knox: if a bad actor breaches the first line of defense and no other precautions exist, they have unrestricted access to do untold damage. However, you can mitigate the damage with a multi-layered defense strategy in place.

When evaluating data, it is critical to understand how it travels and where it is stored. For example, things displayed on Amazon's marketplace may be sold and shipped by third parties. When this occurs, sensitive client data is transmitted to the seller/supplier, who may have less secure data protection, increasing the risk of a breach or other assaults.

2. Conduct security testing to build immediate reaction processes

Cyber-attacks are ongoing and unexpected. As a result, consistent monitoring and testing are required. When vulnerabilities are identified, automation can initiate predefined responses, such as isolating compromised systems, notifying workers, and commencing remediation operations to guarantee that additional assaults are avoided.

Scanning solutions can track transactions, communications, and supply chain activity to detect suspect behavior more quickly. Companies can uncover holes in software, hardware, and network infrastructure, such as unpatched systems, that could be exploited. These initiatives contribute to a more resilient and adaptable defense against hostile attackers. Many incursions can be mitigated or eliminated by proactively detecting and repairing vulnerabilities before they are exploited.

In addition to scanning, you can utilize penetration testing to identify vulnerabilities and red teaming to simulate offensive attacks to assess how your systems will react to prospective cyber-attacks. Together, these tests will reveal hidden flaws and evaluate the efficiency of your present security measures.

3. Encourage a security-first culture

To secure your firm, employees, and consumers, security must be a cultural pillar. Companies should provide training to ensure that staff understand the necessity of high-security standards and are actively involved in sustaining them.

In a supply chain where sensitive information is exchanged between multiple parties, every employee and vendor should be considered part of the security process. Efforts to foster a security-first environment include security threat training, simulated phishing attempts with incentives for employees who demonstrate best practices, and the development of a security policy that includes IT, legal, and procurement team members at all stages of the supply chain.

Promoting a security-first culture raises total awareness and vigilance, involving each individual in the security solution. A top-down commitment guarantees that the appropriate resources are allocated to cybersecurity, lowering the likelihood of gaps that could compromise the supply chain.

This chapter discusses the risks associated with AI supply chains, including vulnerabilities introduced by third-party dependencies. It examines how weaknesses in the supply chain can compromise the security of AI systems. The chapter also outlines strategies for securing AI supply chains, such as thorough vetting of third-party vendors and implementing robust security protocols.

Chapter - 11

AI Security in IoT and Edge Computing Environments

Chapter 11: AI Security in IoT and Edge Computing Environments (NEW)

- The Intersection of AI, IoT, and Edge Computing
- Security Challenges in AI-Driven IoT Devices
- Threats in Decentralized AI Systems

11.1 The Intersection of AI, IoT, and Edge Computing

Data generation is increasing exponentially in today's digital age, where every device—from basic sensors to complex autonomous vehicles—is interconnected. This phenomenon poses considerable issues, including latency in communicating with faraway computers, network congestion, and the energy consumption associated with centralized infrastructures. In this setting, edge computing and artificial intelligence (AI) are emerging as game changers, altering how we process and use information.

Edge computing places processing and decision-making capabilities close to where data is created. This method not only optimizes reaction times but also increases resource efficiency. It is vital in areas such as healthcare, where immediate action is required; industry, which requires constant optimization; and smart cities, which rely on real-time decision-making to improve quality of life. The convergence of edge computing,

AI, and IoT satisfies these requirements while paving the path for a more agile, autonomous, and resilient technological environment.

Edge computing, AI, And IoT

Edge computing is a distributed processing approach that transfers analysis and decision-making skills away from centralized cloud systems and towards devices near data sources. These devices, including advanced sensors, intelligent gateways, and IoT modules, function as network edge nodes, able to conduct complicated activities without needing regular connections to remote servers. This method reduces the transmission of big data quantities to central computers, lowering latency and bandwidth consumption. As a result, system efficiency increases, particularly in applications that require real-time reactions, such as industrial monitoring and energy management.

AI works smoothly with edge computing, providing an excellent environment for performing advanced algorithms. AI embedded in peripheral devices may analyze data locally, discover trends, develop predictions, and make autonomous decisions without needing a cloud connection. This optimizes processes and improves system resilience because many key functions may continue to operate even when connectivity is constrained.

The integration of edge computing, AI, and IoT enables an ecosystem that dynamically adapt to changing environmental conditions, allowing for safer, more efficient, and scalable solutions in industries such as industrial, healthcare, and smart cities. This method revolutionizes technological design and implementation, paving the way for more autonomous and robust systems.

Real-world Applications

The convergence of edge computing, AI, and IoT is transforming numerous industries with practical applications that address specific demands, increasing productivity and enabling real-time decision-making. Here are some significant applications:

Smart Cities and Connected Automobiles

In transportation, IoT modules combine with edge computing and AI to process traffic data in real-time, allowing for congestion identification, route optimization, and improved urban mobility. V2X (vehicle-to-everything) systems powered by 5G networks enable information transmission with millisecond latency, improving road safety by anticipating potentially dangerous circumstances.

This technique helps smart cities optimize their energy consumption. Intelligent public lighting systems employ IoT modules to detect pedestrians or cars and alter lights accordingly, lowering energy consumption and increasing sustainability.

Real-time Monitoring for Healthcare

Wearable medical equipment, such as heart monitors and glucose sensors, use edge computing to process and analyze data locally. This allows for real-time anomaly identification, vital in emergencies without relying on the cloud. Advanced communication technologies are critical in these environments, delivering dependable connections even in places with low coverage.

Furthermore, systems can function independently by processing data locally during connectivity outages, improving resilience and emergency response capabilities.

Industrial Optimisation and Predictive Maintenance

The convergence of powerful IoT modules and AI algorithms at the network edge in industry is revolutionizing predictive maintenance. They measure characteristics such as vibration, temperature, pressure, and edge computing to identify potential failure patterns.

For example, an edge computing system in machinery can identify vibration anomalies and schedule preventive maintenance, reducing unplanned downtime and productivity consequences. 5G connectivity enables real-time data transmission, which improves maintenance through exact synchronization.

Precision Agriculture

Precision agriculture uses IoT, edge computing, and artificial intelligence (AI) to increase yields, optimize resource use, and minimize environmental effects. They measure variables such as humidity and nutrition levels. AI algorithms process this data locally and respond immediately, such as changing irrigation.

Advanced networking technologies transmit data in rural areas, allowing for efficient operation even in remote locales.

Energy Management and Sustainability

Edge computing improves energy management in smart buildings and electric networks. HVAC systems regulate temperature based on occupancy, whereas lighting systems react to available natural light. Edge computing in smart grids enables dynamic electricity distribution control, including managing renewable sources and lowering usage during peak demand.

Retail and Logistics

In retail, IoT sensors and AI-enabled cameras analyze customer behavior in real-time to optimize product placement, adjust prices, and personalize offers. Edge computing enhances inventory management and logistics by analyzing transportation data in real-time. In logistics, IoT modules and edge computing monitor critical conditions, such as the temperature of sensitive products in transit, and automates decisions to preserve their integrity.

The integration of edge computing, AI, and IoT modules, made possible by improved connectivity technologies, is transforming various industries.

11.2 Security Challenges in AI-Driven IoT Devices

The combination of AI and IoT has the potential to completely transform industries by producing smarter, more autonomous systems. AI-powered IoT solutions allow devices to gather, analyze, and act on data in real-time, resulting in improved decision-making, predictive maintenance, and process optimization. Despite the enticing promises, merging AI with IoT poses numerous substantial hurdles. To fully realize the potential of AI-powered IoT systems, these issues must be solved, which range from data management and security concerns to interoperability and scalability.

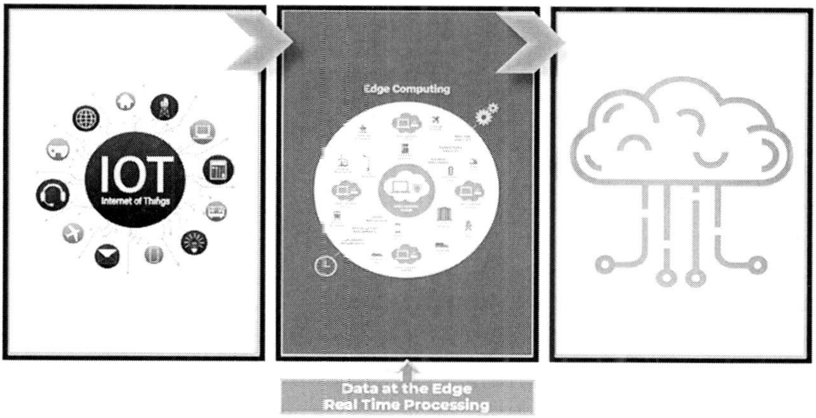

Data Management and Processing

One of the most difficult difficulties in integrating AI and IoT is handling the massive data IoT devices create. These linked gadgets continuously generate real-time data streams, resulting in massive amounts of unstructured data. AI requires huge datasets to train machine learning models, but gathering, storing, processing, and filtering this data can be difficult.

The data supplied by IoT devices is frequently noisy and may require preprocessing and cleaning before AI algorithms can extract useful insights. Ensuring data quality, consistency, and correctness is difficult, especially with large-scale IoT deployments that collect data from many sources. Furthermore, the data must be processed swiftly to allow for real-time decision-making necessitating robust computational infrastructure, either at the edge or in the cloud.

Security and Privacy Concerns

The convergence of AI and IoT increases security and privacy risks. IoT devices are frequently vulnerable to assaults due to flaws in their security systems, and adding AI to the mix broadens the attack surface. AI models rely heavily on data from IoT sensors, and any manipulation of that data — whether through device compromise or man-in-the-middle attacks — can result in inaccurate decisions, potentially leading to dangerous consequences in critical systems such as healthcare or autonomous vehicles.

Additionally, AI algorithms frequently require access to sensitive personal data, such as health or location information, to generate accurate predictions. This presents privacy problems, particularly if the data is shared between various devices and networks. End-to-end security for AI-driven IoT systems is critical, but protecting the device and the data is a significant barrier.

Scalability and Networking Infrastructure

As IoT networks grow, scaling AI solutions to handle larger deployments becomes increasingly difficult. IoT networks frequently include thousands, if not millions, of devices that produce continuous data streams. Training AI models to analyze large amounts of data and give real-time insights necessitates significant computational resources, storage, and bandwidth.

Many AI techniques, particularly deep learning models, are computationally demanding and necessitate significant processing capacity, which IoT devices frequently lack. Cloud-based solutions can help alleviate some of this strain, but sending huge amounts of data to the cloud for processing introduces delay, raises bandwidth costs, and may be impractical for time-sensitive applications.

Edge computing, which processes data closer to the device, has emerged as a solution for local AI computations on edge devices or neighboring nodes. However, putting AI at the edge presents unique issues, such as ensuring that edge devices have adequate processing power, energy efficiency, and the capacity to update AI models as needed.

Interoperability and Standards

The lack of standardization and interoperability between IoT devices and platforms makes AI integration problematic. IoT ecosystems often include various devices that use different communication protocols, operating systems, and data formats. AI systems require easy access to data across different devices to work properly, but a lack of common standards can result in compatibility concerns and data silos. Furthermore, different AI platforms and tools frequently use proprietary algorithms and formats, making adopting standardized solutions across multiple IoT deployment scenarios challenging. Standardizing IoT protocols and AI frameworks is crucial for enabling seamless integration, but this is a continuous problem due to the IoT landscape's diversity and complexity.

Ethical and Bias concerns

AI algorithms are susceptible to prejudice, which becomes a concern when linked to IoT systems that make vital judgments, such as in healthcare, law enforcement, or autonomous vehicles. Bias in AI models can be caused by inaccurate training data or poor algorithmic design, resulting in unequal or unfair outputs. For example, biased AI choices in healthcare IoT systems may deny services to specific groups.

Ensuring that AI models used in IoT are fair, transparent, and ethical necessitates thoroughly evaluating data sources, algorithms, and the ramifications of AI-based choices. This task becomes increasingly difficult as the size and diversity of IoT systems increase.

While merging AI and IoT shows great promise for constructing intelligent, automated systems, various hurdles must be overcome. Managing massive volumes of data, maintaining security and privacy, scaling AI for big networks, solving interoperability challenges, and addressing ethical considerations are all key to the effective implementation of AI-powered IoT solutions. As technologies improve, solving these hurdles will be critical to realizing the full promise of AI-IoT convergence.

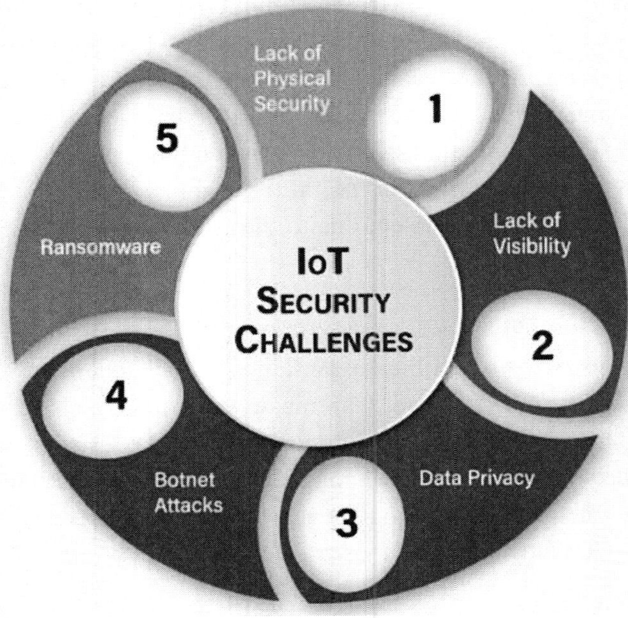

11.3 Threats in Decentralized AI Systems

While decentralized AI provides various advantages and prospects, it also has several threats and constraints that must be addressed. These problems may impact the broad acceptance and efficacy of decentralized AI systems. Let's look at some of the main issues and limitations:

1. Scalability

Scalability is a major difficulty for decentralized AI. As the need for AI computational capacity continues to rise, decentralized systems must be capable of handling the increased burden. The success of decentralized AI depends on the network's ability to expand efficiently and accommodate many users and tasks.

2. Integration with the Current System

Integrating decentralized AI into existing systems can be complicated. Many organizations already have established infrastructure and processes; thus, implementing decentralized AI may necessitate considerable changes and adaptations. Ensuring smooth integration and interoperability with existing systems is critical to effectively adopting decentralized AI.

3. Data Privacy and Security

While decentralized AI seeks to solve data privacy and control concerns, it also introduces new data privacy and security difficulties. Decentralized systems rely on distributed networks, making it more difficult to protect sensitive data. Strong encryption and authentication techniques are required to secure data from unauthorized access and breaches.

4. Governance and Decision-making

Decentralized AI presents issues of governance and decision-making. In a decentralized system, who can make choices and set the parameters of AI algorithms? Ensuring that decision-making procedures are transparent, inclusive, and accountable is critical for fostering trust and preventing power concentration in the hands of a few organizations.

5. Lack of Standardization

The lack of standardization in decentralized AI might cause issues with interoperability and compatibility. Distinct decentralized AI platforms may employ distinct protocols, frameworks, and data formats, making it difficult to trade and collaborate on AI projects. Common standards and protocols can help with interoperability and collaboration in the decentralized AI ecosystem.

6. Energy Consumption

Decentralized AI systems, like their centralized counterparts, require tremendous processing power, resulting in high energy consumption. As the need for AI computing capacity grows, it is critical to find energy-efficient solutions that reduce the environmental effect of decentralized AI.

7. Technical Limitations

Decentralized AI systems may have slower processing rates and less storage capacity than centralized ones. Overcoming these constraints and ensuring decentralized AI systems can execute complicated tasks quickly is critical to widespread adoption and efficacy.

Despite these issues and limits, decentralized AI has tremendous potential to change the AI landscape. By solving these difficulties and capitalizing on the advantages of decentralized AI, we can build a more democratic, inclusive, and equitable AI environment. Collaboration and creativity are critical to overcoming these obstacles and realizing the full potential of decentralized AI.

To demonstrate the challenges and limitations of decentralized AI, examine a real-world example from geek culture. Consider creating a decentralized AI system to analyze and forecast the outcomes of competitive video game matches. This system is designed to deliver insights and techniques to players, coaches, and fans, resulting in a more competitive and enjoyable gaming experience.

However, scalability issues develop when the system is required to manage a significant influx of data from numerous ongoing matches simultaneously. To make accurate predictions, the decentralized network must be able to process and analyze the data in real-time. The effectiveness of the decentralized AI system depends on ensuring that the network can scale efficiently and handle the increasing workload.

This chapter discusses the risks associated with AI supply chains, including vulnerabilities introduced by third-party dependencies. It examines how weaknesses in the supply chain can compromise the security of AI systems. The chapter also outlines strategies for securing AI supply chains, such as thorough vetting of third-party vendors and implementing robust security protocols.

Part – 3:
Defending AI Systems from Cyber Threats

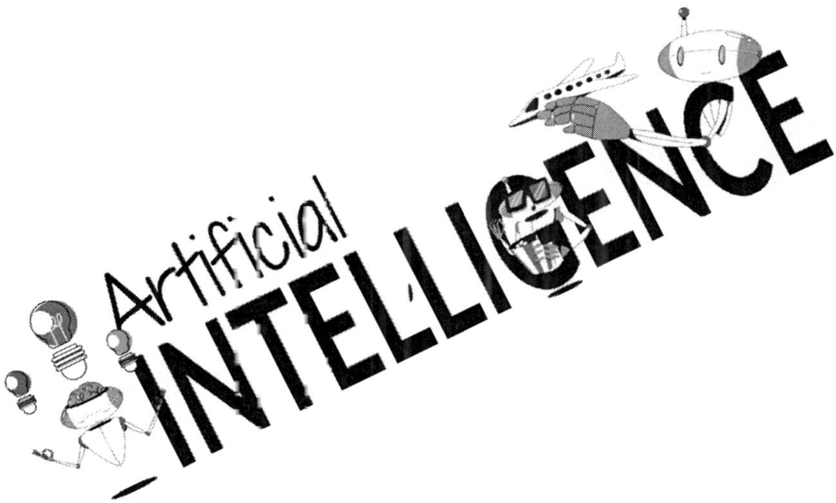

Chapter - 12

Secure AI Development and Deployment

Chapter 12

Secure AI Development and Deployment

- ➢ Best Practices for Secure AI Coding
- ➢ Security-Focused AI Frameworks
- ➢ Implementing AI Model Robustness

12.1 Best Practices for Secure AI Coding

Secure Data Sources and Pathways

Data is used extensively in AI applications to train, test, and refine models and algorithms. As a result, it is critical to guarantee that the data sources and pipelines are secure and reliable. This means you should utilize encryption, authentication, and permission measures to prevent unauthorized data access, alteration, or leaking. You should also check the data's quality, accuracy, and relevancy and eliminate any sensitive or personal information that isn't required for the AI work. You should also record the data sources and pipelines and keep track of the data provenance and lineage to trace the data's origin and history.

Follow the Code Standards and Recommendations.

AI applications frequently use complicated and unique code that is difficult to understand, debug, and maintain. As a result, adhering to coding standards and norms can help you develop clear, consistent, and legible code. Coding standards and guidelines can also help you avoid frequent mistakes, vulnerabilities, and bugs that might jeopardize the security and performance of your AI apps. You should utilize code analyzers, linters, and formatters to check and enforce coding standards and rules. Use comments, documentation, and naming conventions to describe your code's logic and purpose.

Implement security Testing and Validation.

AI applications can exhibit surprising and unexpected behaviors and outcomes, particularly when confronted with novel or adversarial inputs, scenarios, or surroundings. As a result, it is critical to include security testing and validation methodologies that allow you to examine and validate your AI applications' functionality, robustness, and resilience. Security testing and validation methods include unit testing, integration testing, system testing, penetration testing, fuzzing, and adversarial testing. These methods can assist you in identifying and correcting any faults, vulnerabilities, or weaknesses in your code, models, or algorithms, as well as ensuring that your AI applications comply with security needs and specifications.

Implement Secure Deployment and Maintenance Processes

AI applications are neither static nor final items. They must be deployed and managed securely and dependably. This means you should employ secure deployment and maintenance techniques to safeguard your AI applications against external or internal dangers such as cyber-attacks, sabotage, or misuse. Secure deployment and maintenance practices may include using secure servers, networks, and platforms, implementing encryption and access control policies, monitoring and auditing AI activities and performance, updating and patching code, models, or algorithms, and responding to incidents or issues.

Consider the Ethical and Legal Implications

AI applications can have major ethical and legal ramifications for users, stakeholders, and society. As a result, it is critical to address the ethical and legal implications of your AI applications and verify that they comply with applicable laws, rules, and guidelines. You should also adhere to ethical and responsible AI principles and best practices, including justice, transparency, accountability, privacy, and human rights. You should also communicate and engage with users and stakeholders, informing them of your AI applications' aims, capabilities, limitations, and hazards.

Learn from the Community and the Experts

AI is a rapidly expanding and dynamic field with constant new advancements, difficulties, and opportunities. As a result, it is critical to learn from the community and professionals while staying current on the newest AI trends, research, and developments. You should also seek feedback, advice, and direction from other AI developers, researchers, and practitioners, as well as participate in forums, events, and projects that will allow you to increase your skills, knowledge, and expertise with secure coding for AI applications.

12.2 Security-Focused AI Frameworks

OWASP's Top Ten LLM Security Risks

The OWASP Top 10 for Large Language Models (LLMs) lists key vulnerabilities unique to LLMs, such as data leaking, model inversion attacks, and accidental memory. It includes a standardized checklist for developers and security specialists to inspect and safeguard LLMs.

This methodology aids in identifying and addressing the security concerns posed by the use of LLMs in a variety of applications. It promotes secure coding methods, regular vulnerability assessments, and incorporating security measures into the design phase.

Google's Secure AI Framework (SAIF)

Google's Secure AI Framework (SAIF) aims to improve security across AI operations by highlighting the importance of securing AI algorithms and their operational environment. SAIF covers various security measures, from original design to deployment, including encryption techniques, secure user access, and anomaly detection.

This concept also emphasizes the continuity of AI systems, encouraging resilient design that predicts and mitigates faults. The SAIF pushes for regular security evaluations to adapt to evolving risks and ensure that AI systems are reliable over time.

NIST's AI Risk Management Framework

NIST's Artificial Intelligence Risk Management Framework provides principles for addressing the hazards associated with AI systems. It offers a structured approach to risk identification, assessment, and response adapted to specific difficulties, such as algorithmic bias or unexpected behavior. It promotes consistent security policies across all AI applications, increasing transparency.

NIST's approach invites stakeholders to collaborate and share best practices and difficulties, improving collective understanding and AI security.

The Framework of AI Cybersecurity Practices (FAICP)

The Framework for AI Cybersecurity Practices (FAICP), created by the European Union Agency for Cybersecurity (ENISA), is intended to address the security issues raised by integrating AI systems across several sectors. The concept offers a lifecycle approach, beginning with a pre-development phase in which organizations evaluate the breadth of AI applications and identify potential security and privacy threats.

FAICP highlights the importance of data analysis in identifying biases and vulnerabilities, and it suggests developing a governance framework to monitor AI security efforts. In the development and post-deployment phases, the FAICP emphasizes security by design, including secure coding methods, rigorous testing, and transparent AI operations per international standards such as ISO/IEC 23894.

Here are some guidelines for protecting the security of AI systems:

Customize Generative AI Architecture for Better Security

Customizing the architecture of generative AI models can greatly improve their security. This entails creating models with built-in security features like access controls, anomaly detection, and automated threat response systems.

Additionally, implementing regular threat modeling and security assessments during the development phase aids in the early detection and mitigation of threats. This proactive strategy assures that the AI system can withstand attacks and illegal modification.

Harden AI Models

Hardening AI models entails protecting them from adversarial assaults that aim to trick the models into generating inaccurate predictions. Techniques such as adversarial training, which trains models with normal and adversarial data, can improve their robustness.

Implementing defensive measures such as input validation and anomaly detection can also assist AI models in resisting adversarial attacks. These tactics make the models less susceptible to manipulation, ensuring their correctness and reliability in real-world applications.

Prioritize Input Sanitation and Prompt Handling

Input sanitization is essential for keeping harmful inputs from compromising AI systems. This includes verifying and cleansing all data inputs to ensure they are free of potentially dangerous items that could exploit AI model flaws. Establishing strict data validation rules and sanitizing inputs before AI models process them might assist in preventing injection attacks and other harmful behaviors.

Optimizing prompt handling is critical for generative AI systems to avoid exploitation by malicious or misleading prompts. This includes developing tools to recognize and filter out harmful or improper stimuli that could result in undesired outcomes. Using context-aware filtering and establishing strong prompt management procedures helps generative AI systems answer appropriately and safely.

Monitor and Log AI Systems

Continuous monitoring and logging of AI system actions is critical to ensuring security. Organizations can discover and respond to anomalies or suspicious activity in real-time by tracking system behavior and logging interactions.

Automated monitoring technologies that use AI to scan logs and discover strange trends can help improve threat detection capabilities. Regular log reviews and security audits guarantee that potential issues are detected and handled immediately.

Develop an AI Incident Response Plan

An AI incident response plan is essential for successfully handling security breaches and other problems involving AI systems. This strategy should specify methods for detecting, responding to, and recovering from problems while minimizing disruption to operations.

Incorporating clear roles and responsibilities, communication protocols, and recovery methods into the incident response plan enables enterprises to respond quickly and efficiently to AI-related security events. Regularly updating and testing the plan improves readiness for evolving threats, improving overall AI security.

12.3 Implementing AI Model Robustness

What is AI Robustness?

AI robustness refers to the ability of AI systems to execute optimally and reliably under various settings. This notion is more than just preventing AI systems from failing; it is also about ensuring they survive in the face of noisy data, adversarial attacks, or significant environmental shifts. Here's why robust AI is important in today's technology-driven world:

Resilience Against Adversarial Attacks

In an age where cyber threats emerge daily, strong AI systems can detect and defend against attempts to manipulate or deceive them.

Stability in Varying Conditions

Resilient AI systems adapt easily and deliver consistent outcomes when changing market trends or weather patterns.

Enhanced Safety and Reliability

The margin for error is very small in crucial applications such as autonomous vehicles and healthcare diagnostics. Robust AI ensures that judgments are precise and trustworthy, even in uncertain situations.

Understanding AI robustness entails investigating three crucial areas: data variety, model generalization, and adversarial resilience. Each component contributes significantly to AI's resilience against the huge unpredictability of real-world scenarios. Understanding the essence of AI robustness becomes critical as we move toward a future in which AI's role is likely to grow.

AI resilience is the lifeline that keeps AI systems performing consistently, regardless of the obstacles. Consider an AI system as a marathon runner. AI systems must navigate through noisy data, withstand adversarial attacks, and adapt to environmental changes, similar to how runners do.

Importance

This definition emphasizes both the durability and adaptability of AI systems. Why is this so important? Here are some persuasive reasons:

Performance Stability

When confronted with noisy data that can clutter and confuse, robust AI systems distinguish between the important and the irrelevant, preserving their performance integrity. This consistency is critical in high-risk industries such as banking, where real-time choices affect markets and economies.

Protect Against Adversarial Attacks

Cybersecurity threats are an ongoing war in the digital world. AI robustness protects AI systems from being deceived or compromised, ensuring that choices are unaffected by harmful influence.

Adaptability to Environmental Changes

The only constant in our lives is change. Robust AI systems can pivot and adapt to environmental changes, such as changes in user behavior, global climates, or technology breakthroughs.

Thus, AI resilience is more than just a theoretical ideal; it is the foundation of practical, dependable AI applications. It guarantees that AI systems can resist real-world settings' unexpected and frequently chaotic character. As AI evolves and integrates more into the fabric of society, the emphasis on robustness will only grow. AI development has numerous hurdles, including unpredictable real-world circumstances and evolving hostile threats.

Implementation

Robustness in AI systems is a dynamic property that changes over the machine learning lifetime. This lifetime includes everything from initial data collection and model training to AI system implementation and continuous monitoring. Each level brings distinct difficulties and opportunities for increasing robustness, ensuring that AI systems can withstand adversarial attacks, data corruption, and other unexpected weaknesses.

Data Collection

The quality and diversity of training data are critical to the success of any AI model. High-quality, diversified, and precisely labeled datasets are essential for developing strong AI systems. These datasets allow models to learn diverse patterns while reducing the risk of bias, resulting in improved performance stability under various scenarios.

Model Training

At this stage, strategies like adversarial training can dramatically improve model resilience. Developers can uncover and address vulnerabilities early on by exposing AI systems to threats or probable failures while training. This procedure is similar to immunizing the system from future hostile attacks.

Deployment

Once deployed, AI systems must function in the actual world, which is frequently unpredictable and constantly changing. It is critical to ensure that the model works well under ideal circumstances and retains its integrity and performance when confronted with unexpected inputs or conditions.

Ongoing Monitoring

Continuous monitoring and testing after deployment are crucial for ensuring AI robustness. This includes continually analyzing the system for emerging threats and adjusting to changes in the operational environment. It is a proactive approach to security that aims to swiftly discover and correct new vulnerabilities before they may be exploited.

Each of these stages necessitates a well-considered strategy to incorporate robustness into the fundamental fabric of AI development. It is not enough to defend against existing risks; you must also anticipate and prepare for future issues. This iterative method assures that AI systems are dependable, safe, and effective, regardless of the changing landscape of digital dangers and opportunities.

By incorporating robustness into each stage of the machine learning lifecycle, developers and researchers can construct AI systems that function admirably under a wide range of scenarios but also help to improve safe, trustworthy AI technologies.

This chapter outlines best practices for secure AI coding, emphasizing the importance of writing secure and resilient code. It introduces security-focused AI frameworks designed to mitigate risks during development. The chapter also discusses how to implement AI model robustness to ensure that models remain secure and reliable during deployment.

Chapter - 13

AI Security Testing Methodologies

Chapter 13

AI Security Testing Methodologies (Expanded)

- Penetration Testing for AI Models
- Red Teaming AI Systems
- Automated AI Vulnerability Assessment Tools
- Case Studies of AI Security Testing

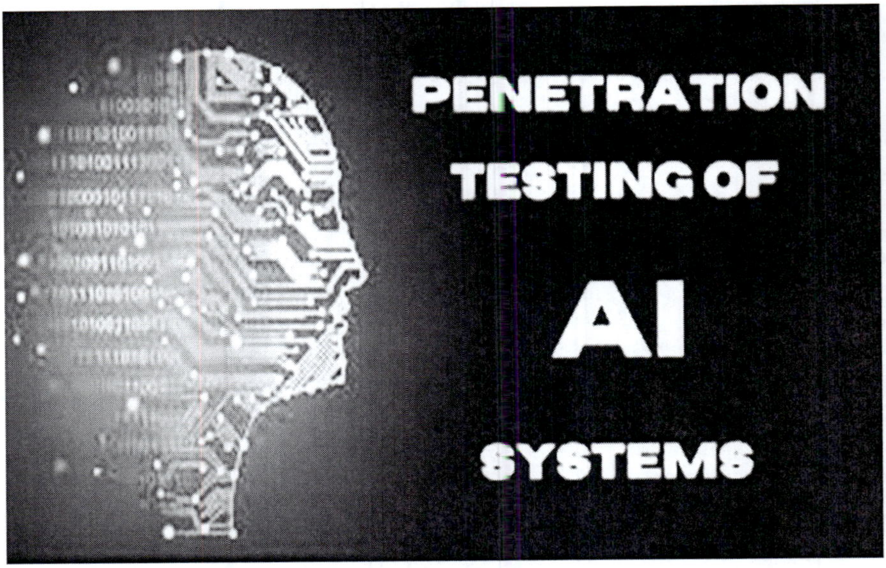

13.1 Penetration Testing for AI Models

Pentering an AI, particularly an LLM, is more challenging than usual. There are numerous undiscovered ways for an AI algorithm to solve a problem while compromising security. To pass these examinations, hackers must have security competence, inventiveness, strategy, and execution skills. This collection of testing procedures is neither exhaustive nor exclusive.

Evaluation of security controls.

Pen testers assess security safeguards such as access limits, encryption, and anomaly detection to ensure that an LLM does not have excessive powers. A tester may attempt to force an AI program to update a database without user agreement, which is considered excessive autonomy. Even after authentication, an AI application should be given only the data it needs.

As a system is only as strong as its weakest link, testers must also look for plugin and extension vulnerabilities in AI systems. After checking for excessive permissions in third-party packages and plugins, hackers can create requests that take advantage of plugin design faults, such as accepting configuration strings instead of parameters.

Pentesters test authentication mechanisms by using username/password, MFA, or OAuth tokens. Like traditional software, AI systems contain privileged accounts that allow administrators, developers, and other high-level users to access specific features or data. These accounts may have access to sensitive data, configuration settings, or AI system behavior. Therefore, hackers may look for credential stuffing or weak password policies.

Verifying Input

Input verification assesses an AI system's ability to handle malicious, unexpected, or defective inputs. The most known example is prompt injection, in which hackers attempt to build inputs to query an LLM to identify situations where inputs are not properly vetted or validated. There are multiple inputs to test because the number and configuration of inputs are limitless, and the results are usually unpredictable.

Pentesters may look at how an AI application handles large or complex inputs, such as those with nested structures or high recursion, which might be used to launch a DoS attack. They also ensure that input data is sanitized to exclude potentially harmful content. Examples include raw SQL injection code and escape character text. Input verification also ensures that plugins filter and handle inputs correctly, preventing local command execution and remote code execution. For example, a plugin may use "ls" to list the contents of a directory. Incorrect input processing in AI models and plugins can allow attackers to inject commands like 'ls; rm -rf /,' which will delete all folder contents if the necessary permissions are granted.

Testers assess LLM infrastructure's durability to high input quantities. Hackers can load-test a system by submitting many requests to simulate a DoS attack and establish resource consumption limits.

Validating Output

AI output can reveal to hackers how the output is processed and what happens to the input. Some short feedback loop tests involve testers evaluating a single input response. Other output verification tests require that a pen tester send multiple queries to elicit incorrect responses and identify vulnerabilities. Pen testers can evaluate LLM output for XSS by inspecting the encoding, filtering, and sanitization. Fuzzing the AI or plugins with erroneous inputs can uncover exploitable vulnerabilities such as RCE or configuration override. In this type of testing, they flood the system with many randomly generated inputs to detect crashes, memory leaks, and security vulnerabilities and then use fuzzed inputs to evaluate the AI's output, behavior, and error-handling systems.

Instead of only analyzing output formatting, testers can also verify content. Historical distortion can deceive AI models. These tests may take longer and involve many inputs to influence the AI's behavior and test various outputs based on new inputs.

Psychological Manipulation

LLMs are not the only ones who can fall victim to security vulnerabilities. Red teams can use social engineering to deceive customers into providing sensitive information or granting unauthorized

AI system access. To collect sensitive data, pen testers may send phishing emails, pretext phone calls, or impersonate authorities or coworkers. Thorough testers may create fake websites and realistic phishing campaigns to lure employees into entering passwords or clicking dangerous links. Social engineering assesses security awareness, as well as suitable rules and procedures.

Simulation of Insider Threats

When security measures fail, threat actors can obtain access to a system, or hostile insiders can abuse their privileges or credentials. To prevent data leaks and model theft, pen testers will ensure that internal users do not have unchecked access to training data, non-anonymized user data, or model internals. Even authorized users should only have the access rights required for their work. Hackers will ensure that its parameters and design are encrypted to prevent attackers from reverse-engineering or replicating an AI model, even with internal access. This highlights inadequate access control, monitoring, authentication, and insider threat detection.

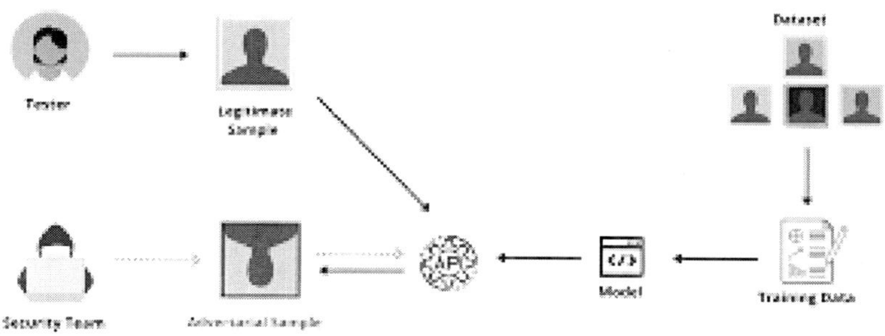

13.2 Red Teaming AI Systems

AI red teaming provides an innovative, proactive approach to enhancing AI while limiting possible risks, allowing enterprises to prevent costly AI catastrophes.

Companies are under pressure to implement generative AI to compete in a global market. To ensure responsible adoption, governmental and regulatory agencies worldwide are meeting to debate and understand the best strategies to address AI risk without limiting innovation. A disagreement exists about how governments can and should control risk through regulation, yet regulation necessitates a thorough understanding of what is being regulated.

You don't know what you don't know about AI at this stage, which challenges how to engage enterprises in conversations about preventing model abuse and security issues. However, some methods are effective. Responsible AI adoption begins with a methodology emphasizing flexibility and continuous development, giving firms a consistent procedure for identifying and addressing AI risks.

AI Red Teaming for Innovation and Dependability

Agencies such as the National Institute for Security and Technology (NIST) have produced frameworks that fit these criteria, allowing enterprises to proactively ensure a more consistent approach to safe and dependable AI implementation. Organizations that adopt these concepts and investigate how to mitigate AI risk can help shape future AI safety policies.

AI red teaming, which incorporates best practices from existing cybersecurity industry frameworks, is assisting in the definition of new best practices for testing the safety and security of models and providing companies with the resources they need to improve the quality of AI adoption and deployment. AI red teaming engagements, in particular, leverage a community of experienced security and safety researchers to identify how models might be abused, allowing firms to detect and mitigate AI risks early on.

Addressing potential misuse channels ahead of time helps firms prevent costly AI incidents that hurt their brand, reputation, and customer trust.

AI Red Teaming Promotes Safety and Security

AI red teaming provides a unique, proactive approach to enhancing AI while limiting potential hazards, which aligns with the US government's objective for responsible AI development. Building on the bug bounty concept, AI red teaming can be organized to reward researchers for the security vulnerabilities and potential misuse scenarios they discover. This strategy promotes a diverse collection of academics to carefully test AI and identify potential vulnerabilities.

Red teaming engagements are primarily concerned with preventing AI systems from producing undesirable results. This might include censoring bomb-making instructions or displaying potentially upsetting or illegal imagery. The purpose here is to identify potential unintended effects or responses in large language models (LLMs) and ensure that developers understand how guardrails must be altered to decrease the model's risks of misuse.

On the other hand, red teaming for AI security is intended to detect faults and security vulnerabilities that could allow threat actors to abuse the AI system and jeopardize the integrity, confidentiality, or availability of an AI-powered application or system. It ensures that AI deployments do not give an adversary a foothold in the organization's systems.

Working with the Security Researcher Community on AI Red Teaming

Companies should collaborate with the AI security research community to improve their red-teaming efforts. They are a team of highly qualified security and AI safety experts who specialize in detecting flaws in computer systems and AI models. Employing them ensures that the most diversified talents are utilized to test an organization's AI. These individuals provide corporations with a new, independent viewpoint on AI implementations' evolving safety and security problems.

Organizations should also establish procedures for close communication between internal and external teams during red teaming engagements to achieve the best results. Furthermore, organizations must think creatively about how to best train and incentivize security researchers to address the organization's most important security and safety challenges. This varies depending on the organization. For example, what is considered dangerous for a bank may not be as significant for a social media chatbot.

13.3 Automated AI Vulnerability Assessment Tools

Vulnerability management identifies, classifies, repairs, and monitors software, network, and computer vulnerabilities. This proactive strategy is critical to many businesses. It protects an organization's digital assets, ensuring their security and dependability throughout time.

Traditional vulnerability management methods are effective at managing vulnerabilities but have inherent flaws. Let's focus on the most notable ones:

Manual Labor

Traditional network vulnerability evaluation relies heavily on manual techniques. These operations take a long time, are susceptible to human mistakes, and are typically inefficient. Manual intervention causes the process to slow down. It increases the chances of disregarding or entirely missing vulnerabilities.

Limited Scope and Velocity

Nowadays, IT infrastructures are becoming larger and more complex. Adapting old techniques may present complications. The manual nature of these procedures restricts their ability to quickly investigate and assess vulnerabilities.

There is no Comprehensive Analysis

Conventional methods focus solely on discovering flaws. They neglect an organization's objectives, infrastructure, and overall context. It may result in ineffective and poorly focused corrective measures.

Response Following Discovery

Reactive operation is the standard for traditional network vulnerability management systems. Their treatment of vulnerabilities is dependent on their identification. It exposes systems to unknown attacks or zero-day vulnerabilities that have yet to be discovered or addressed.

Difficulties in Tracking Novel Threats

Conventional approaches struggle to keep up with newly revealed defects. Finding and resolving new risks becomes challenging when security reports and threat information have to be manually examined, which takes time and effort.

Recognizing these Restrictions is Crucial.

You need to encourage the investigation of sophisticated vulnerability management strategies. They should combine automation, contextual analysis, and real-time threat intelligence. Such advances strive to address these shortcomings and strengthen the security posture. AI is becoming an important tool for managing vulnerabilities in cybersecurity. It improves efficiency throughout all aspects of the process.

AI powered Vulnerability Assessment

AI for network security has transformed vulnerability management. It provides numerous advantages and improves security protocols. Traditional approaches struggle to keep up with the increasing complexity and number of cyber threats. However, AI-powered vulnerability management systems rise to the challenge. They overcome these challenges and revolutionize how vulnerabilities are found, analyzed, and mitigated.

Machine Learning for Vulnerability Detection

Using labeled datasets, supervised learning systems may rapidly identify known vulnerability patterns. It accelerates the identifying procedure. Deep learning algorithms like CNNs and RNNs excel in analyzing complex network data. They aid in detecting small flaws and unusual behavior in complicated networks.

Utilizing Natural Language Processing (NLP) for Security Intelligence

NLP facilitates automated network scanning. It sifted through the material, grouped threats, and ranked them. In addition, NLP aids in the collection and interpretation of threat intelligence from a variety of sources. It identifies insights to prevent emerging dangers.

Network traffic monitoring and behavior analysis. It is critical to monitor network traffic and evaluate behavior. It covers anomaly detection, threat hunting, User and Entity Behavior Analytics (UEBA), and intrusion detection. These tasks are critical to AI-powered vulnerability detection. AI-powered systems analyze network data for anomalies. They offer proactive threat detection and rapid response to potential security breaches.

AI-Enhanced Penetration Testing and Red Teaming

AI automates processes such as surveillance, vulnerability detection, and clever exploitation. These systems replicate real-world cyber-attacks and identify flaws. Furthermore, they employ self-learning and adaptive testing methods. They improve methodologies depending on previous experiences and emerging dangers.

Around every 39 seconds, a new cyber attack appears on the internet. It results in more than 2,200 incidents per day. This is where AI in network defense comes in. It offers faster, more efficient, and more accurate testing methods. AI-driven software testing methodologies are great for obtaining insights into the vulnerabilities discovered daily.

Businesses are increasingly relying on AI to automate vulnerability detection in their networks. Thus, they encounter numerous obstacles and issues that must be carefully considered. One significant barrier is the quality and accessibility of data. Despite the massive amounts of data generated by networks, it is frequently unstandardized, fragmentary, or contains noise. Good, relevant data is essential.

Another issue is the explain ability and interpretability of AI models. These models may excel in identifying weaknesses. To develop confidence and accountability, however, we must first understand how they arrived at their findings. Finding the optimal balance between model complexity and interpretability remains a major concern.

Smooth operation requires seamless integration with existing security tools and workflows. Many firms already use security technologies and procedures. Implementing AI-driven solutions without disrupting operations necessitates careful design and implementation.

Ethical and legal considerations are especially important when using AI to find vulnerabilities. Adherence to legislation such as GDPR is critical, as is confronting moral issues concerning data protection and security.

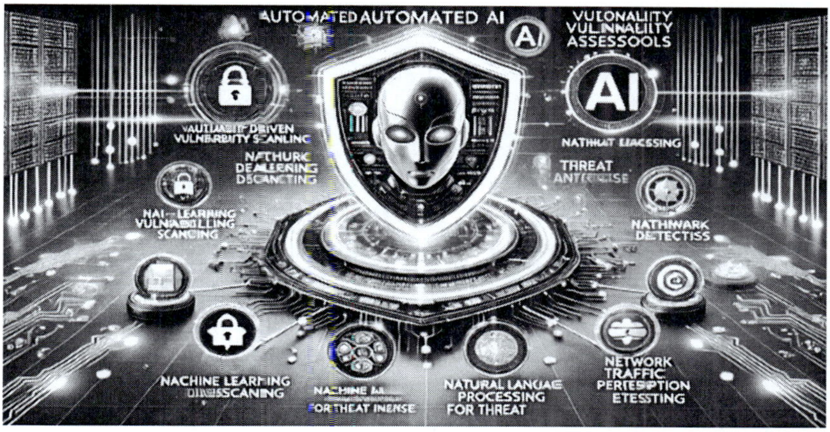

13.4 Case Studies of AI Security Testing

Case Study 1: IBM's Application of AI in Security

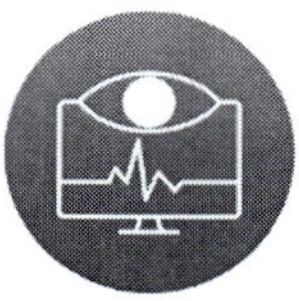

Background: IBM, a global leader in technology and consulting services, has been at the forefront of incorporating AI into its cybersecurity expertise. Faced with the difficulty of detecting and mitigating more sophisticated cyber threats, IBM turned to artificial intelligence (AI) to improve its security operations.

Implementation: IBM's Security Intelligence Operations implemented Watson for Security, an artificial intelligence system that analyzes and interprets large amounts of unstructured data, such as blogs, research papers, and other threat intelligence sources. This technique allows for faster and more precise identification and correlation of possible threats than traditional methods.

Results:

Improved Threat Detection: IBM reported that utilizing Watson for Security reduced the time it took to investigate security events by 60%. The AI system could evaluate and interpret data 50 times faster than human analysts, dramatically accelerating the danger detection process.

AI improved IBM's accuracy in recognizing real positives, reducing the number of false positives by 30%. This enabled security professionals to concentrate on serious dangers rather than filtering through unnecessary notifications.

Scalability:

The AI technology allowed IBM to scale its security operations to tackle the growing number and complexity of cyber threats without requiring a commensurate increase in human resources.

Case Study 2: Microsoft's Application of AI to Cyber Threat Protection

Background: Microsoft, a leading global technology company, faces millions of threats daily across its extensive product and service ecosystem. Microsoft has used artificial intelligence to defend its cloud infrastructure and client data to strengthen its security defenses.

Implementation: Microsoft integrated AI and machine learning algorithms into its security operations via the Microsoft Intelligent Security Graph, which processes over 6.5 trillion daily signals from its products and services. This AI-powered solution uses advanced analytics to detect anomalies, identify threats, and deliver actionable insights to security professionals.

Results:

Rapid Threat Detection and Response: Using AI, Microsoft decreased the average time to detect attacks from 24 hours to less than one hour. AI systems continuously monitor and analyze data, enabling real-time danger identification and rapid response.

Increased Threat Detection Rate: Microsoft's AI-powered security solutions have increased malware and phishing attack detection by 40%. The system's ability to learn and adapt to new threats has proven critical in detecting and reducing previously undiscovered threats.

Preventative Defense Mechanisms: Using AI-enabled predictive analytics, Microsoft was able to anticipate future threats and apply preventative safeguards. This has resulted in a 60% reduction in effective cyber-attacks against its systems.

Case Study 3: Board riders Use AI for Fraud Detection.

Overview: Board riders, a leading action sports and lifestyle firm with brands including Quicksilver, Billabong, and ROXY, encountered substantial issues protecting its global operations. Maintaining strong cybersecurity with a small workforce was critical, with over 700 retail locations, 20 e-commerce sites, and various warehouses worldwide.

AI Implementation: Board riders used Darktrace's Self-Learning AI and Autonomous Response to improve visibility and security across its network and cloud environments. The AI started by learning the regular 'patterns of life' for each user and gadget, which allowed it to recognize tiny variations that indicated potential risks.

Key Results:

Board riders turned Darktrace to completely autonomous mode in a matter of weeks. This enabled Darktrace RESPOND to take independent action against continuing cyber-attacks. The AI's capacity to operate autonomously lowered the time required for the security team to respond to threats, freeing up valuable hours to focus on other security measures.

Ransomware assault: In 2021, Darktrace was the first to respond to an attempted ransomware assault against Board riders. The AI spotted the threat and quickly warned the team using Darktrace's Mobile App. This prompt approach helped to mitigate substantial damage and ensure business continuation.

Cloud Security:

Darktrace now protects the cloud environment of the Board riders, including Microsoft 365. This was especially crucial during the transition to remote and hybrid work since it enabled visibility into account takeovers and other criminal activity across cloud apps.

These case studies from IBM, Microsoft, and Broad riders demonstrate the transformational power of AI in Security testing. These businesses' ability to detect, assess, and respond to cyber threats has been improved through the use of AI. Significant increases in threat detection times, accuracy, and proactive defensive mechanisms illustrate the importance of artificial intelligence in modern security measures.

This chapter explores the various AI security testing methodologies. It explores penetration testing for AI models to identify vulnerabilities and the role of red teaming in simulating attacks on AI systems to assess their defenses. The chapter also covers automated AI vulnerability assessment tools that help detect potential weaknesses, along with case studies showcasing real-world applications of AI security testing.

Chapter - 14

AI Security Metrics and Benchmarking

Chapter 14:

AI Security Metrics and Benchmarking

- Measuring AI Model Robustness
- AI Risk Assessment Frameworks

14.1 Measuring AI Model Robustness

Reliability and robustness in AI are critical for assuring safety, trustworthiness, and equality. As a result, if a company intends to integrate AI into its operations, AI applications must be reliable and robust in order to increase public adoption and progress in AI technologies.

Explain ability and Verification

AI systems should be designed in a way that is transparent and understandable to developers and users. This enables people to grasp how the model works, how its logic and reasoning capabilities work, and what limitations should be considered before employing the AI system.

Model Robustness

Reliable AI uses approaches such as data augmentation, distribution ally robust optimization, and fine-tuning from pre-trained models to improve the robustness of deep learning models. This ensures that the AI system is both reliable and resilient.

Failure Identification and Validation

AI systems may have flaws and failures that degrade their performance. As a result, developers should employ approaches like importance sampling, randomized smoothing, and neural network verification to estimate failure probabilities and evaluate machine learning models. These strategies help to reduce AI model faults and increase their reliability in an enterprise setting.

Uncertainty Quantification (UQ) is an important component of AI systems. UQ seeks to quantify and explain the confidence and robustness of AI models. UQ can help identify sources of uncertainty, such as data noise, model misspecification, or adversarial attacks, and reduce their impact on AI system performance and safety.

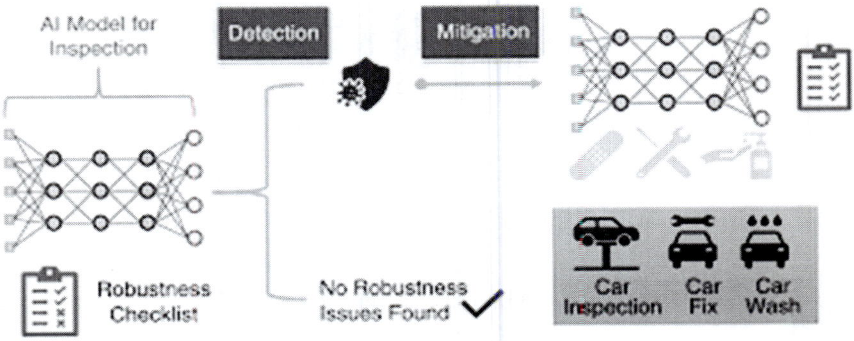

Challenges and Risks for Reliable and Robust AI

One of the primary goals of reliable and robust AI is to develop systems that can perform difficult AI tasks across several domains and contexts while being dependable and resilient to uncertainties and errors. AI provides automation, intelligent analysis, and a variety of visual applications, including Natural Language Processing (NLP) and computer vision. However, implementing such AI objectives in a company is not easy. Despite AI's many potentials and uses, obstacles and hazards arise when designing and implementing AI systems that are not reliable or robust.

The following are some of the problems and hazards related to developing dependable and robust AI:

Safety

AI systems must not hurt humans, animals, or the environment, either purposefully or unintentionally. The safety element of AI is critical for tomorrow's organizations that want to integrate AI ethically. For example, self-driving cars must avoid collisions, medical diagnosis systems must not misdiagnose, and military robots must not endanger civilians or allies. To combat this, AI models should use efficient architecture and include a failure mechanism in case of unforeseen scenarios.

Fairness

Bais is an inherent danger that AI bears. AI systems must not discriminate against or favor specific groups or individuals based on variables such as ethnicity, gender, age, or religion. Bias and disinformation can also have a negative impact on business operations. Biassed hiring procedures, biased credit scoring, and social media censorship are all examples of such hazards. If missed, this can tarnish the consumer-provider relationship, harming the brand's image.

Accountability

Artificial intelligence systems should be developed to justify their activities and judgments. It should be provided with methods and filters that allow AI systems to be held accountable for their actions. This can be shown in the form of a recommender system that justifies its advice or a facial recognition system that reports accuracy. Accountability is vital in AI, as it is in any other impactful technology.

Transparency

Humans must be able to comprehend and interpret AI systems' design and behavior. This not only allows developers to fine-tune the model and execute assessment tests, but it also improves mistake detection when training the AI model. Optimized Transparent machine learning models, interpretable natural language processing systems, and explainable computer vision models are all instances of AI that promote transparency.

14.2 AI Risk Assessment Frameworks

AI risk management considers technological, ethical, and societal factors to guarantee that artificial intelligence technologies are created and used responsibly and safely. An AI risk management framework offers a structured approach to this effort. The AI risk management framework includes the creation of policies and procedures for assessing AI applications for ethical, legal, and technological flaws.

A complete AI risk management framework tackles data privacy concerns, bias, fairness in algorithmic decision-making, and the dependability of AI outputs to assure accountability and compliance with applicable rules. Security experts utilize the approach to reduce risks like adversarial attacks and unintended implications of automated judgments.

Implementing an AI risk management framework is critical for enterprises involved in the development, implementation, and use of artificial intelligence systems. The framework serves to:

1. Protect persons and organizations from potential danger.
2. Ensure ethical and responsible AI development.
3. Users and stakeholders should be able to trust AI technologies.
4. Comply with developing norms and standards.

5. Maximize the benefits of AI while reducing its negative consequences.

Organizations may leverage the power of AI while protecting themselves from potential negative outcomes by building a strong AI risk management framework.

AI risk management systems, while differing in their specific methodologies, have certain critical components for effectively addressing the issues provided by AI technologies. These components are the foundation of a complete risk management plan.

Risk Identification and Assessment

Any AI risk management system is built on the capacity to identify and assess potential hazards. The method entails doing a thorough analysis of an AI system's design, functionality, and potential consequences. Organizations must evaluate not only technological risks but also ethical, social, and legal consequences.

Risk detection frequently requires collaboration among multiple teams, including data scientists, domain specialists, ethicists, and legal professionals. They may employ approaches like scenario planning, threat modeling, and impact assessments to identify potential dangers.

Once identified, risks are typically evaluated for their likelihood and potential impact. The evaluation aids in the effective allocation of resources and risk prioritization. However, risk assessment in artificial intelligence is a continuing process. The dynamic nature of AI systems and their operational contexts makes them vulnerable to the emergence of new dangers over time.

Governance and Oversight

Effective AI risk management necessitates strong governance frameworks and distinct lines of accountability. It should center on establishing roles, responsibilities, and decision-making processes inside an organization.

AI governance components include a

1. board-level AI ethical committee.
2. Chief AI officer or comparable executive position
3. Cross-functional teams are responsible for implementing risk management procedures.
4. Clear escalation channels to address identified concerns

Governance frameworks should also specify how AI decisions are made, documented, and evaluated. Defining how AI-related decisions are made entails creating protocols for approving high-risk AI initiatives and developing principles for responsible AI development and implementation.

Transparency and Explain ability

The emphasis on openness and explain ability guarantees that AI decision-making processes are as transparent and understandable as possible for stakeholders, including developers, consumers, and those affected by AI judgments.

Transparency entails being upfront about the data used, the methods employed, and the system's constraints. Explain ability takes a step further by attempting to provide accessible explanations for AI judgments or suggestions.

Techniques to Improve Transparency

1. Use interpretable machine learning models whenever possible.
2. Implement Explainable AI (XAI).
3. Provide detailed documentation of AI systems' objectives, capabilities, and limitations.
4. Establish systems for stakeholders to request explanations for AI choices.

Fairness and Bias Mitigation

Addressing issues of fairness and prejudice are essential components of AI risk management. AI systems may accidentally replicate or even magnify societal prejudices, resulting in unfair outcomes for certain populations.

Fairness in AI is a multifaceted term that can be defined and quantified in a variety of ways. Organizations must carefully assess which fairness measures are most suited to their specific use cases and stakeholders.

Bias Mitigation Strategies

1. diverse and representative data collection procedures.
2. Regular audits of AI systems for biased outcomes.
3. Implementing algorithmic fairness strategies.
4. Working with affected communities to identify and correct any prejudices.

Privacy and Data Protection

Because AI systems frequently rely on enormous volumes of data, including personal information, maintaining privacy and compliance with data protection standards is critical. Data compliance focuses on protecting individual privacy rights while allowing for the beneficial use of data in AI development and implementation.

Important Aspects of Privacy and Data Protection in AI

1. Implementing data minimization principles.
2. Ensuring safe data storage and transmission.
3. Obtaining informed consent for data usage, where applicable.
4. Complying with relevant data protection requirements (e.g., GDPR, CCPA).
5. Employing privacy-preserving AI approaches such as federated learning or differential privacy.

AI systems are susceptible to security vulnerabilities such as data poisoning, model inversion attacks, and adversarial instances. Security measures are critical for protecting AI systems from hostile attackers and ensuring their dependable operation.

Security Considerations for AI Risk Management

1. Keeping training data and models safe from illegal access or alteration.
2. Implementing strong authentication and access controls.
3. Consistent security testing and vulnerability assessments
4. Creating incident response plans for AI-related security breaches.
5. Ensure the integrity of AI decision-making processes.

Human Oversight and Control

While AI systems can provide great capabilities, effective human monitoring and management are required to minimize risks and assure responsibility. This component of the paradigm focuses on establishing the appropriate balance between AI autonomy and human judgment.

Human Oversight Mechanisms

1. Clearly stated human-in-the-loop procedures for crucial choices
2. Regular human assessment of AI system outputs and judgments.
3. Ability to override or disengage AI systems as needed.
4. Training programs to guarantee that human operators grasp AI systems' capabilities and limits.

Risk assessment Frameworks

The NIST AI Risk Management Framework (AI RMF)

The National Institute of Standards and Technology (NIST) AI Risk Management Framework is a voluntary advice document intended to assist enterprises in addressing risks associated with the design, development, use, and evaluation of AI products, services, and systems.

Key Features:

Four central functions Govern, map, measure, and manage.

1. The emphasis is on a socio-technical approach, understanding both technological and societal components of AI concerns.

2. Ability to adapt to varied organizations and AI applications.
3. Focus on trustworthy AI features, such as validity, reliability, safety, security, and resilience.
4. The framework offers a systematic yet adaptable approach to AI risk management, allowing enterprises to modify it to their individual requirements and settings.

EU AI Act

The European Union's AI Act is a regulatory framework designed to protect the safety and basic rights of EU people while dealing with AI systems.

Key Features:

1. The risk-based approach divides AI systems into four risk levels: unacceptable, high, limited, and minimal risk.
2. Prohibition of some AI practices considered to pose unacceptable hazards.
3. High-risk AI systems must meet stringent standards such as risk management, data governance, human monitoring, and transparency.
4. Establishing a European Artificial Intelligence Board to enable deployment and push standards.

The EU AI Act, which was passed on May 21, 2024, is projected to have a substantial impact on AI development and deployment internationally due to the EU's legislative power.

IEEE Ethical Aligned Design (EAD)

The Institute of Electrical and Electronics Engineers (IEEE) Ethically Aligned Design principles provide a comprehensive framework for emphasizing ethical issues in autonomous and intelligent systems.

Key Features:

Emphasis on human rights, well-being, data agency, efficacy, openness, accountability, and knowledge of abuse. The EAD framework is notable for its heavy emphasis on ethical considerations and its global, forward-thinking attitude.

MITRE's Sensible Regulatory Framework For AI Security

MITRE's Sensible Regulatory Framework for AI Security seeks to develop guidelines and best practices for improving the security and resilience of AI systems.

Key Features:

1. Integrates technical, operational, and organizational factors to ensure comprehensive AI security.
2. Focuses on detecting and addressing the most serious dangers connected with AI systems.
3. Encourages collaboration among the government, industry, and academia to share knowledge and best practices.
4. Encourages the continuous review and adaption of security measures in response to changing threats and technological advances.

The framework provides a solid foundation for enterprises looking to protect their AI systems from a variety of dangers while still encouraging innovation and operational effectiveness.

MITRE's Atlas Matrix

MITRE's Adversarial Threat Landscape for Artificial-Intelligence Systems (ATLAS) Matrix provides a thorough overview of potential AI threats.

Key Features:

1. Provides a complete analysis of adversarial tactics, methods, and procedures (TTPs) for AI systems.
2. Customizes danger information for specific AI application fields, such as healthcare, finance, and autonomous systems.
3. To guard against recognized dangers, particular countermeasures and best practices are recommended.

4. encourages parties to share threat intelligence and defensive strategies.

The ATLAS Matrix is a powerful tool for understanding and mitigating adversarial threats to AI, assisting enterprises in developing more secure and robust AI systems.

This chapter focuses on measuring the robustness of AI models through security metrics, helping to evaluate their vulnerability to attacks. It also introduces various AI risk assessment frameworks designed to assess and mitigate risks, providing a structured approach to ensuring the security and reliability of AI systems.

Chapter - 15
Future-Proofing AI Against Cyber-Attacks

Chapter 15:

Future-Proofing AI Against Cyber-Attacks

- Emerging Threats in AI Security
- Quantum Computing and AI Security Risks
- Preparing for the Next Generation of AI Threats

15.1 Emerging Threats in AI Security

Generative AI can be exploited for nefarious purposes, offering significant security hazards. One of the most alarming risks is the creation of deepfakes, which are very realistic but false images, videos, or audio recordings that can be used to propagate misinformation, manipulate public opinion, or blackmail individuals. Cybercriminals can also employ generative AI to create more convincing phishing emails or social engineering assaults, making it easier to deceive and exploit their targets. Furthermore, AI-generated code can be used to create advanced viruses or automate large-scale cyber-attacks.

The availability of generative AI tools enhances these dangers by allowing even non-experts to make destructive content. To combat these concerns, strong rules must be implemented, AI technology must be monitored, and countermeasures must be developed to detect and prevent the misuse of generative AI for malevolent purposes.

Model Theft

Model theft poses a significant issue in the field of generative AI, as unauthorized individuals or entities can steal, reproduce, or misuse AI models. These models frequently require a significant investment of time, resources, and experience, making them important intellectual property for businesses. If a model is stolen, competitors can get an unfair advantage, or criminal actors can utilize it to generate damaging applications such as disinformation or advanced cyber threats.

Furthermore, once a model has been taken, it can be reverse-engineered, allowing the thief to retrieve critical data or proprietary processes hidden within it. This not only weakens the security and privacy of the data used to train the model, but it also jeopardizes the organization's competitive advantage. To prevent model theft, it is critical to install strong security measures such as encryption, access limits, and monitoring, as well as legal safeguards such as patent and copyright rights. These methods serve to assure the security of AI models, as well as their controlled and ethical use.

Bias and Discrimination

Bias and discrimination are important problems in terms of generative AI hazards. These algorithms can accidentally detect and exacerbate existing biases in the data on which they are trained. If an AI model is trained on biased data, it may give unfair or biased results, such as preferring certain groups over others in decision-making processes like hiring. For example, if a generative AI used for job screening is trained on data including previous biases, it may unfairly disadvantage particular demographics.

Similarly, AI-generated content may contain stereotypes or discriminatory words without trying to. These issues might have a harmful impact on the actual world by promoting social disparities or stereotypes. To avoid this, it is critical to carefully pick and handle training data to remove bias, to routinely test AI models for fairness, and to monitor the content they generate. Including various viewpoints in the creation of AI systems is also critical for recognizing and resolving any biases. By following these safeguards, organizations can help to guarantee that generative AI supports fair and equitable outcomes.

Adversarial Attacks

Adversarial assaults pose a significant hazard in the context of generative AI, in which malevolent actors purposefully modify input data to fool or mislead AI models. These assaults consist of producing subtly altered inputs, such as manipulated graphics or text, that appear normal to humans but lead the AI to make inaccurate or damaging decisions.

For example, an adversarial attack could lead to an AI model misclassifying an image misinterpreting a stop sign as a speed restriction sign, which could have major ramifications in self-driving cars. Adversarial attacks on generative AI might result in the generation of false or dangerous content, jeopardizing the AI's output dependability and safety. These attacks target vulnerabilities in the AI model's learning process, exposing loopholes that cybercriminals might exploit.

To fight against adversarial assaults, it is critical to create strong AI models that can withstand such manipulations, test models on a regular basis with adversarial situations, and put in place security measures that identify and prevent these types of attacks. By doing so, enterprises can ensure the integrity and trustworthiness of their generative AI systems.

Robustness and Reliability Issues

Ensuring resilience and dependability in generative AI is a big challenge, as these models often struggle when exposed to unexpected or new inputs. Although generative AI models are powerful, they might give unexpected or inaccurate answers, particularly when dealing with scenarios outside of their training data. This lack of robustness can lead to incorrect outputs, potentially harming or misleading results in real applications.

When confronted with unknown scenarios, an AI model employed to generate legal documents may provide erroneous or incomprehensible material, posing significant legal or financial risk. Furthermore, the model's sensitivity to tiny changes in input data can yield inconsistent and untrustworthy results.

To address these difficulties, it is critical to do extensive testing, maintain constant monitoring, and create fail-safes to ensure that the AI operates consistently across a variety of scenarios. Without addressing these robustness and dependability challenges, generative AI's effectiveness and safety in crucial activities may suffer dramatically.

Lack of Transparency and Explain ability

A major difficulty with generative AI is its lack of openness and explain ability, which makes it difficult to grasp how these models generate their output. Generative AI, particularly those that use deep learning techniques, frequently functions in a "black box" environment, where the decision-making process is obscured and difficult to understand.

This lack of clarity can lead to trust concerns, particularly in high-risk industries such as healthcare, finance, and legal services, where understanding the logic behind choices is critical. Without transparency, it is difficult to determine the veracity of the AI's results or uncover potential biases and inaccuracies. This can lead to unforeseen outcomes or misuse of the technology. To foster trust and assure ethical use, it is critical to develop methods for making AI processes more intelligible, allowing users to see and trust the reasoning behind the AI's judgments.

Regulatory and Compliance Risks

Navigating regulatory and compliance issues is a major concern when adopting generative AI systems. As these technologies rapidly advance, rules and regulations struggle to catch up, resulting in a complex legal landscape. Organizations that utilize generative AI must traverse a variety of regulations governing data protection, intellectual property, and ethical use, which can range significantly among locations and industries. Noncompliance with these standards can result in legal penalties, financial losses, and reputational damage.

Furthermore, a lack of clear criteria for AI use can create uncertainty, making it difficult for businesses to guarantee that their AI activities are completely compliant. This uncertainty is exacerbated by the likelihood that AI-generated content will violate copyright laws, disregard data protection regulations, or distribute biased or damaging information, increasing regulatory risks even further. To mitigate these risks, firms must stay current on evolving rules, implement solid compliance policies, and ensure that their AI systems are developed and operated within legal and ethical constraints.

Organizations can prevent legal concerns and maintain stakeholder trust by communicating with authorities on a regular basis and adhering to best practices.

15.2 Quantum Computing and AI Security Risks

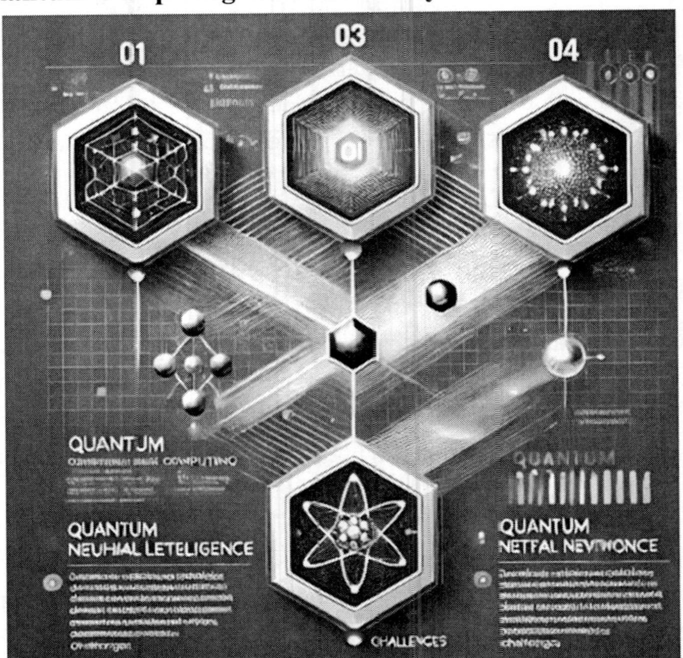

There are significant distinctions between quantum AI and regular AI, the most notable of which is how datasets are processed and analyzed.

While quantum AI has far more powerful data analysis capabilities because it works with quantum computers, classical AI is far more limited in contrast.

Here are some of the main distinctions between these two systems:

Limited Availability

It is critical to recognize that, despite their widespread appeal and wonderful outcomes, quantum sensors and computers are relatively uncommon when compared to classical computing. Furthermore, because they are still in their early stages and are not widely used, the cost of accessible solutions can be prohibitively expensive.

More organizations will eventually employ quantum AI solutions, rendering traditional AI systems obsolete; yet, for the time being, the traditional system remains the business norm.

Complex Data Analysis

There are some tasks that each artificial intelligence system is superior at. For example, quantum AI excels at working with complicated data sets that classical AI struggles with. This is because quantum computing enables the solution of the most complicated problems in seconds, and the utilization of quantum qubits in various states allows for parallel data analysis.

However, certain organizations may face a hurdle because quantum AI works best with algorithms intended to maximize the performance of a quantum computing system. This necessitates the creation and development of new algorithms to handle qubits and other components of these advanced systems.

Inaccurate Results

Quantum AI, like generative artificial intelligence, transforms business activities on a massive scale that a regular computer cannot comprehend. However, they, like generative AI, require human supervision because they are prone to producing incorrect findings. The majority of these faults are due to external influences on the qubits. Companies that implement error-correction strategies and quality checks can protect their reputation among clients while also providing superior solutions.

Several dangers arise from the unsupervised deployment of quantum AI, including ethical issues, environmental hazards, safety risks, and the possibility of bias. To guarantee that the development of these instruments proceeds smoothly, adequate checks and balances that allow for long-term growth must be established.

Some of the typical risks associated with quantum AI implementation:

Environmental Risks

It is crucial to remember that quantum computers require a significant amount of energy to function properly, and widespread use of these instruments may generate environmental and health risks if not properly regulated.

Sustainability concerns are intensifying as quantum AI, advanced language models, deep learning models, and deep learning solutions improve. While it is critical to enable technological improvements, it is equally important to ensure that they do not jeopardize natural resources.

Cybersecurity Risks

With the increased demand for quantum computers, cyber security threats have the ability to spread and inflict significant damage to a variety of enterprises and their security systems. Unfortunately, existing cryptography and encryption strategies cannot compete with quantum technologies, which can readily crack practically every encryption algorithm used by cybersecurity professionals today.

If threat actors can leverage the capabilities of quantum computing and distort it to benefit their malevolent intents, quantum algorithms may jeopardize critical user data, resulting in significant privacy breaches. This will make it difficult to evaluate DNNs, and each web contact will be fraught with cybersecurity dangers.

Potential for Bias

AI bias is a genuine thing and a big disadvantage of current technical breakthroughs. The use of quantum machine learning algorithms that create and work with erroneous predictions and data is becoming more widespread because their algorithms are not well-defined enough to detect bias without human intervention.

To verify that quantum AI algorithms are free of prejudice, gender discrimination, and racial bias, they must be tested repeatedly with multiple teams. This reduces the risk of offending the sentiments of a certain consumer group.

Ethical Risks

Quantum intelligence is one of numerous significant AI advances this decade that represent a danger to humans' decision-making abilities. This is especially worrisome when considering the uses of quantum AI in medical, security surveillance, finance, and even the military.

After breaking passwords, these programs may simply breach current security systems and gain access to financial and private information. This increases the requirement for effective surveillance, supervision, and legislation around the broad usage of quantum AI. Furthermore, every solution must be conceived and developed to serve the broader public and not put society at risk.

15.3 Preparing for the Next Generation of AI Threats

Artificial intelligence has evolved from a science fiction dream to a reality, revolutionizing industries and changing the fabric of our lives, work, and relationships with the world. It is transforming almost every aspect of human life, from self-driving automobiles to virtual assistants. However, such tremendous opportunities come with nearly equal risks and challenges connected with AI. The future of AI will be fashioned by an ideal balance of innovation and caution.

Job Displacement

AI will create new job prospects and sources of wealth, but it will also eliminate thousands of occupations, primarily in manufacturing and manual or repetitive work, such as data entry clerks. Customer service and transportation roles are rapidly becoming automated, potentially leading to a significant increase in unemployment if governments and industry do not actively endeavor to reskill and upskill displaced personnel. AI is reshaping high-skilled careers in healthcare, law, and education. These are more difficult to fully automate since they require human empathy and judgmental decision-making. The difficulty will be to guarantee that workers learn the skills required to complete new AI-augmented roles.

Bias and Discrimination

AI systems inherit the biases of the data on which they are taught. AI can perpetuate biases based on race, gender, or socioeconomic status, as shown in hiring, policing, and healthcare. Predictive police algorithms, for example, have been chastised for disproportionately targeting minority areas, reinforcing disparities. This risk necessitates responsible AI development, clear protocols, and rigorous management to ensure that the AI system does not exacerbate discrimination.

Ethical and Autonomous Decision-making

In an era where AI makes judgments in healthcare, law enforcement, or autonomous driving, questions of ethics, responsibility, and human oversight arise. Such scenarios raise extraordinary concerns about the future, such as self-driving cars deciding between life and death for their passengers, aligning AI decisions with human values, and AI-powered drones engaged in combat. More recently, there has been a dispute regarding who is liable when AI systems make a mistake or inflict damage. Thus, effective regulation will be required for accountability in the decision-making process of AI systems in order to protect and prevent persons from violating ethical standards.

Data Privacy and Security

The most significant issue with AI is that it feeds on massive volumes of data, raising substantial worries about data privacy and security. Unauthorized or stolen personal data can result in identity theft, financial fraud, and, ultimately, mistrust of digital networks. However, increased monitoring, social media analysis, and recognition have raised new concerns about the loss of privacy rights.

Even worse, AI systems can be hacked. A hacker could discover ways to exploit holes in AI algorithms and influence outcomes, which is quite concerning, especially when it comes to crucial industries such as health, banking, and national security.

Weaponization of Artificial Intelligence

One of the most terrifying aspects of AI is its potential for conflict. The possibility of killing autonomous weapons, which use AI and may act without human oversight, is a terrifying prospect for unpredictable and uncontrollable warfare. If international regulations governing the use of AI in conflict are not developed, the growth of these technologies poses a direct threat to world security. They have the potential to fall into the wrong hands of rogue nations or terrorist organizations. Thus, weaponizing AI must be one of the critical global partnerships that must be worked out in terms of more cooperation.

Balancing Opportunities and Risks

It is both promising and risky, necessitating collaboration among governments, tech corporations, and civil society to strike a balance between the risks and rewards that AI can bring to humanity. Ethical norms and clear legal frameworks for AI development are the keys to navigating this new frontier. There will be a large demand for investment in education and workforce development to provide people with the necessary skills and experience to adapt to an AI-driven future. Transparency in AI systems will also help to address concerns about bias, ethics, and accountability. Proper regulation and oversight of AI technologies will be required to ensure that they are used responsibly and for the greater good.

This chapter explores emerging threats in AI security, including the potential risks posed by quantum computing. It discusses how quantum advancements could challenge current AI security measures. The chapter also provides strategies for preparing for the next generation of AI threats, emphasizing proactive security measures to future-proof AI systems against evolving cyber risks.

Conclusion

The Evolving Cybersecurity Landscape in AI

Understanding AI technology is critical for cybersecurity experts. As AI evolves, fraudsters might utilize its powers to create more sophisticated attack strategies, offering new difficulties to cybersecurity experts.

Artificial intelligence-driven cyber threats are a developing worry. Cybercriminals use AI algorithms and machine learning techniques to automate their attack procedures, allowing them to carry out large-scale and highly targeted attacks with little human participation. These AI-powered threats have adaptive and evasive tendencies, making them difficult to identify and resist using typical security methods.

One example is the deployment of artificial intelligence-powered malware. Cybercriminals use AI algorithms to construct sophisticated malware that avoids standard security measures by constantly changing its behavior and escaping detection. This malware may change its assault patterns based on real-time observations and replies, making it extremely effective at entering systems and extracting critical data.

The rise of AI-powered cyber-attacks has considerably boosted the demand for cybersecurity personnel with AI competence. Organizations require personnel with a thorough understanding of AI technology and its potential uses in cybersecurity. With this knowledge, these professionals can study AI-driven attack trends, create sophisticated defenses, and deploy strategies to combat evolving cybersecurity and AI threats.

To combat AI-driven cyber assaults, cybersecurity professionals must stay up to date on the newest AI technology advances and understand their implications for cybersecurity. To effectively detect and mitigate AI-powered threats, they must have a strong understanding of machine learning, data analytics, and AI algorithms. Furthermore, a thorough understanding of AI allows cybersecurity specialists to turn the tables on hackers by using AI tools and techniques to improve their defensive capabilities.

AI Challenges for the Cybersecurity Landscape

As AI becomes more available, fraudsters are developing new ways to exploit its capabilities, allowing them to launch complex assaults. One major worry is how thieves use AI to automate and optimize cyber operations. AI algorithms can swiftly scan large volumes of data, discover trends, and produce targeted assaults with little human intervention. However, even hackers must guarantee that their code is working, indicating that AI-based cyber-attacks are not yet completely autonomous.

Despite the need for human oversight to ensure malicious code functions properly and hides hackers' identities from authorities, AI's level of automation allows cybercriminals to launch large-scale, coordinated attacks that they would not have been able to carry out otherwise. These assaults have the potential to penetrate networks, steal valuable information, or cause major infrastructure disruptions.

While AI creates new difficulties in the field of cybersecurity, it also provides significant tools and solutions that can help cybersecurity professionals detect and prevent threats. Understanding how to employ cybersecurity and AI together can provide IT professionals an advantage in the AI arms race against hackers. Given the value of their particular knowledge, it may also make them more desirable for higher-level jobs.

Improved threat detection.

One significant application of AI in cybersecurity is the use of machine learning algorithms to detect threats and anomalies. AI models can evaluate large volumes of data from a variety of sources, such as network logs, user behavior, and system events, to detect patterns that indicate prospective threats. AI-powered systems can detect suspicious activities and warn cybersecurity professionals, enabling for rapid response and mitigation.

AI can also help automate regular and time-consuming processes, freeing up cybersecurity teams to focus on more complicated and vital duties. For example, AI can automate the examination of security alerts, lowering the workload on analysts and allowing them to devote more time and expertise to researching and responding to high-priority occurrences. Given the possible volume of warnings generated by modern networks, automation can improve productivity and keep security operations manageable.

AI can also improve threat intelligence capabilities by automating the collection, analysis, and dissemination of security-related data. AI-powered systems may detect new threats, trends, and indicators of harmful activity without the need for human intervention by monitoring a variety of sources, including social networking sites and hacker-populated dark web forums. This important knowledge allows cybersecurity professionals to proactively adapt their defenses and remain ahead of changing threats.

Improved defenses and response times

Another key advantage of AI-powered systems is their ability to evaluate and correlate data in real time, giving security personnel with actionable insights and context during an active security incident. By swiftly determining the scope and severity of an attack, cybersecurity professionals may respond quickly, establish containment measures, and reduce the effect of a breach.

In addition, cybersecurity pros can employ AI to manage vulnerabilities and patch them. By examining multiple characteristics of a system, its code, and historical data, AI-powered systems may discover potential vulnerabilities and prioritize them depending on their severity and potential impact. This prioritizing allows organizations to focus on correcting the most serious vulnerabilities first, decreasing the window of opportunity for attackers.

Cybersecurity specialists can also utilize AI in user behavior analytics (UBA) to detect strange or inexplicable user activity and assess whether they are cyber dangers. AI systems can detect deviations that signal malicious intent or compromised accounts by creating models based on predicted user behavior. This proactive approach enables firms to discover possible vulnerabilities, such as unauthorized access via underutilized channels, and reduce any damage.

The Value of Continuous Cybersecurity Education

As additional chances to mix cybersecurity and AI capabilities emerge, cybersecurity experts who understand this technology will become increasingly valuable across businesses. In such a quickly evolving sector, being current on the newest AI-driven threats, vulnerabilities, and protection techniques is critical. Continuous learning enables cybersecurity experts to adjust their techniques and remain ahead of cybercriminals who exploit AI for nefarious objectives.

Professionals can broaden their expertise and employment options by pursuing additional schooling that builds on the particular knowledge and skills they've gained as cybersecurity specialists. Furthermore, continual education helps professionals grasp the ethical implications of AI in cybersecurity, allowing them to traverse complicated issues while using and implementing AI technology.

Call to Action for AI Security Professionals

Artificial intelligence (AI) has proven to be a valuable asset in combating cybersecurity threats, allowing the creation of Intelligent Agents to successfully solve specific security difficulties. An Intelligent Agent, whether hardware or software, is intended to maximize the likelihood of achieving a specific goal through its ability to observe, learn, and make intelligent judgments. These Intelligent Agents can discover flaws in complicated code structures, abnormalities in user login patterns, and even new varieties of malware that defy traditional detection methods.

Under the hood, Intelligent Agents process massive volumes of data to learn and comprehend patterns. When deployed in defense systems, these agents use their understanding to analyze incoming data, including previously unknown information.

The Role of AI in Cybersecurity for Professionals

AI in cybersecurity helps security experts identify complicated data patterns, make meaningful recommendations, and enable autonomous mitigation. It improves threat detection, facilitates decision-making, and accelerates incident response.

AI uses three main approaches to address complicated security issues:

Pattern Insights

AI is particularly good at spotting and classifying data patterns that humans may find difficult to examine. It offers these patterns to security experts for further investigation and analysis.

Actionable Recommendations

Intelligent Agents make actionable recommendations based on recognized patterns, guiding security experts on relevant measures.

Autonomous Mitigation

Some Intelligent Agents can operate on behalf of security professionals to address and resolve security vulnerabilities.

While a business may already have competent security personnel, advanced tools, and well-established processes, Intelligent Agents seek to improve and supplement these resources, hence strengthening overall defense capabilities. The first stage in protection is often to uncover vulnerabilities or defects that attackers could exploit. AI-powered source code scanning improves accuracy, resulting in fewer false positives and allowing developers to discover security flaws before deploying applications in production.

Another area where AI can help security professionals is in response to threats. Advanced AI systems deliver threat intelligence and contextual details to the security incident response team. This context enables the team to respond effectively and efficiently to threats, hence improving overall incident response skills.

AI's involvement in cybersecurity goes beyond traditional ways, transforming how businesses protect their systems and data. By combining AI and cybersecurity, security professionals gain access to improved detection, proactive threat mitigation, and intelligent automation, helping them to remain ahead of cyber threats in an ever-changing landscape.

Final Thoughts on Securing AI for the Future

The benefits of AI for businesses are limitless, and industries of all sizes are getting involved, from cybersecurity to financial institutions to government, among others. One thing is certain: this appetite is not going to taper down anytime soon. Securing AI is vital to its acceptance, and it is currently adopting the shape of a pyramid.

The quickly developing nature of AI innovation is creating a scenario in which security solutions must be as agile and sophisticated as the dangers they confront. The only method to secure AI in this fashion is at the inference layer, which requires a comprehensive solution that spans three major areas:

Defense

Strong defense measures are essential. This comprises input validation and sanitization to protect against prompt injection attacks, output filtering to reduce hazardous content production, and runtime monitoring to detect odd activity. Understanding the exact use case is critical, as each application will have different security requirements. Furthermore, considering cross-cutting attacks that target the entire AI pipeline is critical.

Offense

Effective red teaming is critical for detecting vulnerabilities in opaque foundation models and the apps that rely on them. This includes adversarial testing, investigating potential attack vectors, and devising mitigation techniques. This proactive approach enables enterprises to keep ahead of new vulnerabilities and assure the resilience of their AI systems.

Governance, regulations, and compliance (GRC): Navigating the changing regulatory landscape is an essential component of AI security. Every state and industry vertical will have their own set of laws and regulations. While adhering to the "paper defense" is crucial, it is also critical to adopt real security procedures that turn these standards into tangible protection